LAST DAYS OF THE REICH

Count and Countess Folke Bernadotte and their son, Bertil

LAST DAYS
OF THE REICH

The Diary of Count Folke Bernadotte,
October 1944–May 1945

Count Folke Bernadotte

Introduction by Sune Persson

Frontline Books, London

Last Days of the Reich:
The Diary of Count Folke Bernadotte, October 1944–May 1945

This edition published in 2009 by Frontline Books,
an imprint of Pen & Swords Books Limited,
47 Church Street, Barnsley, S. Yorkshire, S70 2AS
www.frontline-books.com

ISBN: 978-1-84832-522-7

Publishing History
Last Days of the Reich was first published by Cassell (London, 1945)
under the title *The Fall of the Curtain: Last Days of the Third Reich*
and by Alfred A. Knopf (New York, 1945) under the title
The Curtain Falls: Last Days of the Third Reich. It is published here
by Frontline Books, London, with a new Introduction by Sune Persson
and Foreword by Bertil and Folke Bernadotte.

A CIP data record for this title is available from the British Library.

For more information on our books, please visit
www.frontline-books.com, email info@frontline-books.com
or write to us at the above address.

Printed in the UK by the MPG Books Group

Foreword

In recent years it has become more and more common to criticise Folke Bernadotte for overstating his own contribution and importance in the White Buses operation. The criticism has been promoted by historical researchers such as Lord Dacre and others, on television and radio as well as in books and the daily press.

These attacks have been responses to the account which our father provided in the diary which forms the core of this new book. His account was originally published under the title *The Fall of the Curtain* but has been re-titled *Last Days of the Reich* for this edition. As an example of this criticism the historian Folke Schimanski recently wrote in *Svenska Dagbladet* that, 'Folke Bernadotte created his own legend in the book *The Fall of the Curtain*, without acknowledging the work of anyone else,' and that 'he over-emphasised his own input.'

We, Folke Bernadotte's descendants, feel it is high time to step in with what we regard to be the true background to our father's book, which was published in June 1945, in other words, hardly two months after the actual events about which he writes.

It is our hope to provoke an understanding of the then prevailing circumstances, thus avoiding these unworthy and fallacious attacks by serious researchers in the future.

Many historians have come to regard our father's book *The Fall of the Curtain* as an historical document, thereby giving it a weightiness which was neither its purpose nor intention. Through our mother we heard how the book came into being.

When the news of the accomplishments of the White Bus mission became publicly known, Norstedt's Publishing Company urged our father to write down an account of his experiences.

At that time he was heavily involved in his Red Cross work concerning emergency relief in Europe and had scarcely the time to write a book. The publishing company's representative Ragnar Svanström, helped out. He, in fact, became Folke Bernadotte's ghost writer for the book and much of its contents and writing should be attributed to him. Naturally, Svanström was not very cognizant with the work of various other people who were instrumental in the success of the mission (e.g.

Ditleff, Günther, Storch, Kersten, Dr. Holm and many others).

Our mother told us that our father was eager to honour numerous others who were involved and had contributed with ideas and proposals but Svanström did not agree. He argued that the material would become too extensive and that the publication of the book would be greatly delayed as the other people's permission would have to be sought and obtained and manuscripts revised, etc. 'They will have to write their own books, Folke. You must write what you yourself experienced.'

Time was of the essence for the publishing company if they were to strike whilst the iron was hot. Through this easy solution the work was simplified and the book – which should be considered more as a journalistic account, rather than an historical document – could be in the shops barely six weeks after the end of the war, to the enormous advantage of the publishing company.

Our father was not at all happy that much of the other people's contributions were diminished. In the end a compromise was agreed. By way of introduction Folke Bernadotte states, 'It is with much hesitation that I, after many requests, have written an account of my experiences during my work in connection with the activity of the Swedish Red Cross in Germany in the last months of the Second World War . . . The account is based on my notes and reports during my travels in Germany from the middle of February to the end of April of this year.'

With regard to criticism of Folke Bernadotte having exaggerated his own accomplishments whilst diminishing those of others, if this criticism had been made during his lifetime, it is more than certain that he himself would have explained the circumstances surrounding the book, but this opportunity was denied him by an assassin's bullet in Jerusalem in 1948.

Bertil and Folke Bernadotte, 2009

Introduction

Count Folke Bernadotte

Count Folke Bernadotte of Wisborg was born in 1895. His father, Prince Oscar Bernadotte, was the son of Oscar II, King of Sweden (1872–1907) and of Norway (1872–1905; Sweden and Norway were in union from 1814 to 1905). Bernadotte was not an intellectual but he was of a decidedly practical disposition. He became a cavalry officer and a good organizer. However, from an early age he had health problems. He suffered from gastric ulcers and recurrent internal bleedings which forced him to leave the Swedish Army in 1930. His later attempts to become a businessman failed. Given his deep religious faith, humanitarian work became more natural for him. In 1943 he became the Vice Chairman of the Swedish Red Cross. Its Chairman, Prince Carl, a close relative of Bernadotte, was eighty-two years old, so Bernadotte became the *de facto* acting head of the Red Cross.

In 1928 he had married Estelle Manville, the daughter of a wealthy American businessman. For the rest of his life, Bernadotte was staunchly pro-American. In spite of this, in Sweden he never played a political role. In elections, he voted for the Conservative Party. In the international arena, he combined a conservative philosophy with a faith in Swedish neutrality, Nordic solidarity and a strong opposition to Communism and the Soviet Union. Bernadotte became internationally known when he directed the exchange of disabled German and British and American war prisoners in Göteborg (Gothenburg) during 1943 and 1944. Later on he was thanked for this when he met the British Foreign Minister, Anthony Eden, and the Allied Supreme Commander, Dwight D. Eisenhower.

The White Buses
For obvious geopolitical reasons, the Swedish Red Cross, together with the International Red Cross Committee in Switzerland, was the only neutral humanitarian organization that could effectively render assistance to all those millions of women and men who were the victims of the atrocities committed by Hitler's Nazi Germany.

In the final stages of the Second World War,

Sweden began to take active steps to secure the release of Norwegian and Danish prisoners in Germany. These efforts were directed by Christian Günther, the Swedish Foreign Minister. Most of the planning, however, was done by the Norwegians. Among them was Niels Christian Ditleff, Ambassador to Stockholm of the Norwegian exile government in London. In February 1945, Folke Bernadotte, a good friend of Ditleff, was appointed leader for a Swedish Red Cross relief expedition to Germany.

On March 12th, 1945, the first column of Swedish buses, painted white and bearing large red crosses – 'the white buses' – drove across the Danish border into Germany. Serving in the expedition were 250 Swedish Army officers and soldiers, as well as Red Cross nurses, handpicked by Bernadotte. The Swedish relief effort involved constant personal risk. During these months, Allied forces were closing in from the west and from the east. Nazi-controlled territory was rapidly shrinking. Large-scale Allied bomb attacks occurred daily. Miraculously, only one Swede in the rescue expedition was killed.

By VE (Victory in Europe) Day, in May 1945, the Swedish Red Cross expedition had saved more than

17,000 prisoners from Germany giving them their freedom in Sweden. From April, this was in fact a Swedish–Danish expedition, and more than half of the 'White Buses' were then Danish. Some 8,000 Norwegians and Danes were saved, but the largest national contingent rescued were some 6,000 Polish citizens. More than 4,000 of those saved were Jews, most of them Polish Jewesses, liberated from the concentration camp in Ravensbrück

Six weeks after the end of the war, in June 1945, Bernadotte's book, *The Fall of the Curtain: Last Days of the Third Reich,* was published. This was his own account of his harrowing experiences in the dying days of Nazi Germany. The amazingly short time it took to publish the book was due to the fact that his ghost writer, Ragnar Svanström, merely printed out Bernadotte's five successive reports to the Swedish Red Cross and to the Swedish Foreign Ministry, while Svanström himself added a few passages, bridging Bernadotte's own accounts.

Bernadotte's book was an international success, translated into eighteen languages and published as a series of articles in the British newspaper the *Daily Telegraph*. Bernadotte became world famous. Ralph Hewins, a British correspondent in Stockholm, later wrote that there were two conceivable candidates for the leadership of a future United States of Europe: Winston Churchill and Folke Bernadotte.

1948: United Nations' Mediator on Palestine

On May 20th, 1948, the United Nations appointed Count Bernadotte as its mediator on Palestine. However, at that time the world's main attention was focused on the Cold War between East and West and, shortly after, on the Soviet blockade of Berlin. A Third World War was looming on the horizon. In the Cold War, Bernadotte's sympathies lay on the American–British side. Hitherto, Bernadotte's work had focused on Europe and North America. Palestine would be his first, and deadly, encounter with the Middle East.

In resolution 186 of May 14th, 1948, the General Assembly empowered the UN Mediator on Palestine, *inter alia,*

- to use his good offices with the local authorities to promote a peaceful adjustment of the future situation in Palestine;
- to co-operate with the Truce Commission appointed by the Security Council;
- to invite, with a view to promoting the welfare of the inhabitants, the assistance of specialized

agencies of the UN and of the International Red Cross.

This was the first time that the UN intervened directly in a political conflict and also the first time it had appointed a mediator to resolve it. However the resolution gave the UN mediator no resources whatsoever to enforce his views.

Against all odds, Bernadotte succeeded in arranging for a four-week truce in the Palestine war, effective from June 11th. After a new round of Arab–Israeli fighting, Bernadotte gave a vigorous speech to the UN Security Council. Then on July 15th the Security Council, for the first time in UN history, *ordered* a new, indefinite, truce in Palestine.

The truce arrangements in Palestine had to be supervised by a mechanism set up by the mediator. The concept of UN peacekeeping missions did not yet exist. Nevertheless Bernadotte, in a short time, starting from scratch, succeeded in building a small truce-supervision body. This was the beginning of United Nations Truce Supervision Organization (UNTSO), still an important UN tool in Middle East peacekeeping operations.

Another of Bernadotte's accomplishments was his handling of the refugee issue. As early as in his first plan, signed June 27th, he suggested 'the right of the residents of Palestine . . . to return to their homes without restriction and regain possession of their property'. In the practical field, Bernadotte, with his vast experience of Red Cross work, initiated the humanitarian relief programme for Palestinian Arab refugees. This marked the beginning of the United Nations Relief and Works Agency for Palestine Refugees in the Near East (UNRWA), which is still at work.

In order 'to promote a peaceful adjustment of the future situation in Palestine', Bernadotte presented two plans. The first, dated June 27th, 1948, suggested that Palestine – defined as the Mandate of 1922 and thus including Transjordan – should form a union, comprising two 'Members'. The City of Jerusalem would be in the Arab territory. The June 27th plan was rejected by both sides. The Arabs were totally against any kind of a Zionist state in Palestine. Israel also flatly rejected Bernadotte's suggestions, stating that no encroachment upon the free sovereignty of the State of Israel was acceptable. Especially objectionable to the Israelis was the mediator's handing over Jerusalem to the Arabs. Bernadotte from now on was a hated man in Israel.

In Bernadotte's second plan, signed on September 16th, the mediator recognized the Jewish state as a reality. The whole of Galilee, he suggested, was to be defined as Jewish territory. Arab–Palestine was still to be merged with Transjordan and the whole of Negev was to be given to the Arab state. The city of Jerusalem was to be placed under UN control. Bernadotte had now made major changes to reconcile the Israelis, but the Jewish state would have covered only some twenty per cent of Palestine. The main winner would still be King Abdallah of Transjordan – and indirectly the King's British allies.

The total rejection of Bernadotte's first plan had been a hard lesson. The mediator had now realized that the United Nations Organization would render him no substantial, military, assistance. Thus, while preparing his second proposal, Bernadotte received two extremely secret visitors, one from the British Foreign Office and one from the US State Department. Bernadotte's second plan now secured support from the two main Western powers. It represented the first joint UK–US action programme on Palestine since the 1920s. The UK–US master plan was to be presented by the UN mediator, as 'made in

Sweden', to the UN General Assembly. The British and American governments were then to ensure that the Arab and Israeli authorities acquiesced in the mediator's recommendations. Thus the Palestine question would be solved, enabling the Western powers to focus all their efforts on the Berlin crisis and the looming threat of a Third World War with the Soviet Union.

However on the following day, September 17th, Folke Bernadotte was assassinated in an ambush in the Israeli-controlled sector of Jerusalem. The murderers were never found and no one was ever convicted of the assassination. It is now well established that the assassination was carried out by members of the Lohamei Herut Yisrael (LEHY), or the Stern Gang. The decision to kill the UN mediator was taken by the LEHY Central Committee, which included Yitzhak Yezernitzky-Shamir. (Shamir later on served as Prime Minister of Israel in 1983–84 and 1986–92). LEHY saw Bernadotte as the main obstacle to an Israeli annexation of Jerusalem and to Jewish control of *all* Palestine.

The Aftermath

The assassination of the UN mediator in Palestine sent a shock wave around the world. Memorial services were held everywhere. Yet no UN sanctions or practical actions against Israel were ever undertaken. Both in Israel and in the Arab states respect and trust for the UN vanished. Furthermore, Bernadotte's second plan was defeated when US President Truman, against the line of his own State Department, publicly repudiated Bernadotte's proposals in a pro-Israeli declaration on October 28th, a few days before the US presidential elections.

Soon the verbal attacks against Folke Bernadotte began. Already in 1945, after the extremely swift publication of his book *The Fall of the Curtain,* important personalities felt offended, since their own contributions were downplayed by Bernadotte. This was the case with the Swedish Foreign Minister, Günther, and with the Norwegian minister in Stockholm, Ditleff, but also in general with the important Norwegian and Danish contributions to the success of the relief expedition. No one heeded the subtitle of Bernadotte's book: *My* humanitarian negotiations in Germany. They probably did not know that his publisher, Svanström, had explicitly advised Bernadotte only to tell *his own experiences.*

The main attack, however, came from Felix Kersten, a masseur with Finnish citizenship. Kersten had been Heinrich Himmler's private physician since 1940, also treating other high-ranking Nazi leaders. In spite of this, in 1943 Kersten was allowed to leave for Stockholm, on condition that he returned to Himmler every fourth month. From then on, the Swedish Foreign Office, and Günther himself, used Kersten to promote Sweden's humanitarian efforts in German-controlled territories. In 1945, Kersten applied for Swedish citizenship. Günther supported Kersten in this, while Bernadotte refused to help. This led to a deterioration in the personal relations between Bernadotte on the one hand and Günther and Kersten on the other. Bernadotte, like the new Swedish Foreign Minister from July 1945, Östen Undén, regarded Kersten as a pro-Nazi collaborator. Kersten was denied Swedish citizenship until 1953. He grew increasingly bitter and in his memoirs, published in various languages from 1947, he viciously attacked Bernadotte as an anti-Semite, and represented himself as the prime mover of the Swedish rescue expedition in 1945. In 1953, Kersten presented a letter from Bernadotte to Himmler, allegedly written in March 1945, stating that Jews were not welcome in Sweden. The Swedish authorities immediately realized that this letter was a forgery. This was also corroborated in 1978 by Scotland Yard, finding that the letter in fact was written on Kersten's own typewriter!

However, Kersten's case was now taken up by the well-known British historian Hugh Trevor-Roper (later Baron Dacre of Glanton). In 1947 Trevor-Roper published his famous book *The Last Days of Hitler*, where Bernadotte was given a very marginal role. This led to an unpleasant correspondence between Bernadotte and Trevor-Roper. At the beginning of the 1950s, Trevor-Roper came to Sweden and visited Kersten. In 1953, relying entirely on Kersten's own narratives, Trevor-Roper publicly attacked Bernadotte in *The Atlantic Monthly*. He gave Kersten sole credit for the success of the 1945 rescue expedition, while Bernadotte was reduced to 'a transport officer, no more'. Trevor-Roper also reiterated Kersten's statement that Bernadotte was an anti-Semite. The article raised a storm of protests in Sweden. When Kersten's memoirs were published in English in 1956, Trevor-Roper, in his introduction, repeated his accusations against Bernadotte. As evidence, he now also used Bernadotte's alleged March 1945 letter to Himmler, adding, in a modest footnote, that the letter's 'authenticity has not been proven'. Trevor-Roper never had the opportunity to apologize to Bernadotte. Later, in 1983, Trevor-Roper's reputation as a serious historian was undermined when he vouched for the authenticity of the so-called *Hitler Diaries*, soon to be proven as not very skilful forgeries.

However the damage to Bernadotte's reputation was now done. Those who murdered Bernadotte in 1948, and other right-wing Israeli extremists, gladly used Kersten's and Trevor-Roper's writings, and sheer lies, to represent Bernadotte as an anti-Semite, thus exonerating themselves from their cowardly deed.

Worse, the Swedish authorities seem to have been silenced over these attacks against Bernadotte. True, a Swedish white book in 1956 defended Bernadotte and likewise totally rejected Trevor-Roper's writings. Since then, for many years, there has been almost total official silence in Sweden around Bernadotte. But winds are changing even in Sweden. In 2002, the Swedish government inaugurated an agency dedicated to international conflict and crisis management, with a focus on peace operations, and named the new agency 'The

Folke Bernadotte Academy'. In 2005, the Swedish Red Cross, at last, made a move and opened The House of Humanity in Malmö, intended as the Swedish Red Cross national centre for humanitarian issues, and explicitly built to preserve the heritage of the White Buses expedition in 1945. In 2007, close to this centre, a monument honouring the brave Swedes and Danes who saved Norwegian and Danish prisoners in 1945 was solemnly presented by the President of the Norwegian Parliament to the King of Sweden. The beautiful monument was financed by donations collected by grateful Norwegian War Veterans and, too in part, by the Danish Red Cross. In Spring 2008, important Swedish personalities demanded that the Swedish government break its silence and also honour Count Folke Bernadotte, the assassinated UN mediator on Palestine.

Sune Persson, 2009

Preface

It is with much hesitation that I, after many requests, have written an account of my experiences during my work in connection with the activity of the Swedish Red Cross in Germany in the last months of the Second World War. I have overcome my hesitation in the hope that what I have told may throw some light on the dramatic events at the time of the collapse of the Third Reich.

The account is based on my notes and reports during my travels in Germany from the middle of February to the end of April this year.

Stockholm,
June, 1945.

LAST DAYS OF THE REICH

My plane left Bromma Airfield, heading West, one day at the end of October, 1944. My destination was Paris, via London. In Paris I was to confer with Allied representatives regarding Sweden's share in post-war reconstruction and other problems. Paris was again a free city in a free land, and one could even at that period safely prophesy that the life of the Nazi empire would be not a thousand years, but little more than a decade.

There are two episodes during my visit to Paris in autumn of 1944 which I shall always recollect with especial pleasure. One was my meeting with General Eisenhower, the other a luncheon where the Swedish Consul-General in Paris, Raoul Nordling, was one of the guests.

On a lovely autumn day, October 2nd, my plane landed on a military airfield at Versailles, where the Allied GHQ had been established. I was immediately conducted to the Supreme Commander's office, where the General, a powerfully-built man, in his fifties, received me with the unaffected friendliness and absence of side which is characteristic of Americans in high positions.

I had been in charge of the organization concerned with the internment of American airmen who had made forced landings in Sweden, and it was on the suggestion of General Curtis, United States Air Force, who had been to Sweden in connection with this, that I visited the Supreme Commander.

General Eisenhower impressed me enormously. I felt here was a man of real greatness, a personality as vital as it was generous and warmhearted. He gave one the feeling of being relaxed and calm, with complete confidence in his ability to reach his goal and carry out the gigantic task he had undertaken. Here, I felt, was a man who knew what he wanted and had the ability to get it. One of his most striking characteristics was his strong sense of humour, which was seldom absent during our talk and gave a charmingly 'human' touch to his personality. The General is very human, and very humane. He expressed no hate of those who had been his antagonists in the Second World War – and certainly none for the enemy's military leaders.

His subordinates are unanimous as to the complete absence of any rigid militarism in their Supreme Commander. This, perhaps, offers the explanation of his greatest quality; the magnificent ability with which he has preserved the team-spirit among the Western Allies, and, often under conditions of great delicacy, adjusted and co-ordinated the sometimes conflicting wishes expressed from various quarters.

General Eisenhower began his talk by expressing his general appreciation of what I had been able to do for American airmen in Sweden, and then went on to discuss the general situation. I was pleased to observe that he had a friendly understanding for Sweden's political attitude. However that may be, he stated in the course of this talk that he was of the firm opinion that Sweden's neutral policy had been the right one, not only from her own point of view, but also from that of the Allies. This was an opinion which I encountered during several of my conversations with representatives of the British and American High Commands. General Eisenhower then discussed with me the question of how and where Sweden could most effectively assist in the post-war problems.

I informed him that I had had a preliminary discussion with representatives of UNRRA, and that the Swedish authorities and the Swedish Red Cross were anxious to hear the views of Shaef. I mentioned that in certain quarters of UNRRA doubts had been expressed as to whether the offers of assistance by neutrals would be favourably received. Eisenhower strongly rejected this opinion, and insisted that all offers of assistance would be accepted. Personally, he said, he thought it very natural that neutral countries should wish to take part in the task of restoration. He wished the occupied countries to establish their own administrations as soon as they were liberated, after which they would be regarded and treated as sovereign states with whom neutral organizations could deal direct and plan post-war action.

Regarding Germany, General Eisenhower stated that the Allied Supreme Headquarters would only collaborate with a single organization covering all the zones of occupation. When I asked him for his opinion concerning Poland in this respect, he thought it would be only right if, for example, the Swedish Red Cross approached the Polish authorities to ascertain their wishes, but that the Russian authorities would probably expect to be consulted. He emphasized, however, that he was not in possession of detailed information regarding plans in Eastern Europe.

I was very struck by the atmosphere at Eisenhower's Headquarters. It was gay and friendly, and there were many signs of the never-failing American sense of humour. When I was shown round I saw a bust of Göring in a niche, which the Germans had forgotten in their precipitate flight. There it stood, but the face was turned towards the wall. 'He's a bad boy,' said my guide, laughing, 'he must stand in the corner until he says he is ashamed of himself.' Among those with whom I had lengthy talks was General Spaatz, chief of the Allied Strategic Air Forces. One of his remarks impressed itself on me. 'When, sometimes during the quiet hours of the night, I think about the appalling destruction my forces cause in Germany and among the civilian population, I have to make myself dwell on the suffering of the French people at the hands of the Germans. Only that thought makes it a little less painful to deal such blows at harmless people in Germany.' General Spaatz said he had never observed any hatred for the enemy in the American or British forces.

In one of the rooms at Supreme Headquarters I noticed a map on which were indicated the various zones of occupation in Germany as planned at that period of the war. There were three main zones. One line, from Lübeck, following the course of the Elbe towards the East, showed the Western boundary of the planned Russian zone. North-western Germany was to be under British occupation, and the South-west under the Americans.

However, I felt that here was a matter which was no concern of mine, and I refrained from asking any questions. I had come to Paris to discuss matters concerning Sweden's humanitarian mission and for no political purposes.

The following day, November 3rd, I attended a lunch given at the Hotel Bristol by the Swedish Chargé d'Affaires, Belfrage. Among those present were my two travelling companions, Doctor Ulf Nordwall, Medical Adviser in Post-War Problems to the Swedish Red Cross, and Baron Erik Leijonhufod, Secretary to the Swedish State Committee for Post-War Relief. And then there was our Consul-General Nordling. I must admit that this man fascinated me. His enthusiasm was as irresistible as it was inspiring. Of course I had read in the papers about Nordling's magnificent contribution to the liberation of Paris. I knew that he had played a highly important part as negotiator between the Allied Forces and the French Underground Movement on the one hand, and the German Occupational Authorities on the other.

Nordling is an old Parisian Swede filled with a deep love of France and the French, and a passionate desire to be of help to the vast number of those who so heroically carried on the struggle for their country's freedom. His activities were sometimes misunderstood. It was necessary to maintain contact with the enemy as well as with the Underground Movement, and this gave rise to suspicions which have since shown themselves to be entirely without foundation. As we sat over our lunch he told us in his frank vivacious way of his many adventures and experiences during the days preceding the liberation of Paris. What especially interested and thrilled me was his account of how he had been able to prevent large numbers of women and men from being deported to Germany, and how he had succeeded in persuading the Germans to release a number of Frenchmen who had been imprisoned in France at the time of the capitulation of Paris. Nordling is not a civil servant who fears responsibility and takes cover under regulations and instructions, but fearlessly acts on his own responsibility. Without these qualities he could never have succeeded in his self-imposed mission. As I listened to him, I became infected by his enthusiasm. I asked myself if I couldn't do something similar for those who were languishing in German concentration camps. Thus a seed was sown in me which was to grow into the expedition of the Swedish Red Cross into Germany in the Spring of 1945.

STOCKHOLM

December, 1944.

Seated in the plane which was carrying me home, my mind was occupied with the project to which Raoul Nordling's talk had given rise. I asked myself would it be possible for Sweden to do something to lessen the suffering caused by the German system of concentration camps, to save at any rate some unfortunates otherwise doomed to die in horrible conditions? I felt little optimism, since I was well aware that the German authorities had firmly rejected all suggestions from the

International Red Cross, as well as from the Red Cross organizations of belligerents and neutrals that they should be allowed to bring relief to the unfortunates in concentration camps. The Germans absolutely declined to allow any foreigner a glimpse into these infernos, as we feared them to be. Nor could we refer to any international agreement, for when the Geneva Convention was drawn up, in 1929, nobody had then thought of incarcerating political suspects in concentration camps. It was reserved for Nazi Germany to conceive this diabolical idea. The concentration camps were well guarded. No one forced behind those grim walls could escape, and no independent observer could enter, lest the dark secrets of this grim system be fully revealed. Of one thing I was convinced. It would be useless to negotiate with any but the most highly placed in the Nazi hierarchy. I knew that if anything was to be done, it must be done without delay. For some time there had been rumours, which could not be ignored, that the German authorities had the intention of 'liquidating' the prisoners in concentration camps if there should be a collapse in Germany's defences, thus ridding themselves of dangerous witnesses.

These were my thoughts on my return to Stockholm, and just as was the case in Paris, it was an encounter with one person which became of decisive importance to the execution of my scheme. This time it was a distinguished Norwegian diplomat, M. Ditleff, a man of sixty, who had served his country in many important posts, and was at the time attached to the Norwegian Legation in Stockholm. It was he who suggested to me that the most important task would be to persuade the Nazi authorities to allow Norwegian civilians to be released from the camps in Germany and evacuated to Sweden. The idea appealed to me greatly, for it was very much on the same lines as Consul-General Nordling's activity, but on a larger scale. M. Ditleff and I went deeply into the question, and arrived at the conclusion that to be successful it would be necessary to contact the Head of the SS, Reichsminister Heinrich Himmler. In such matters final decision rested with him A somewhat encouraging factor was that he was known to have expressed a liking for the Scandinavian countries and their peoples. There was perhaps a faint hope that he might give his approval to our project.

The next thing to do was to confer with the

Swedish Red Cross, and with the Swedish Government. I knew that the latter had for some time been anxious to be of assistance to the Scandinavians imprisoned in Germany. Our Legation in Berlin had transmitted many requests for the liberation of individual prisoners. Our Minister, Arvid Richert, had been untiring in his efforts, which had been by no means fruitless. As is known, he had succeeded in obtaining the release of a number of Norwegian students who had been returned to Norway. This fact was brought up during the ensuing discussions in January and the beginning of February, but it was agreed that it was far more difficult for a Chef de Mission than for a private individual to make contact with those in authority over the concentration camps. As a diplomat he could only attempt such approach through the channels of the Ministry of Foreign Affairs, with the risk that it would end in a cul-de-sac of official non-co-operation and never reach Himmler. When the Swedish Foreign Office instructed me to make an attempt to obtain the release of Norwegian civilians, a plan was agreed on.

At the request of the Swedish Minister, Richert, the Red Cross sent an expedition to Berlin at the time when my discussions were taking place. The object of the expedition was to collect and send home the numerous Swedish-born women who had married Germans, and now found themselves homeless and with no near relations. This gave me an excellent pretext for a visit to Berlin. On my departure by plane, on February 16th, it was officially announced that I was going to inspect the Red Cross expedition to ascertain if it required reinforcing in order to carry out its task. The real object of my visit to Berlin was, of course, to endeavour to meet Himmler and obtain his consent to the internment in Sweden, not only of the Norwegian, but also of the Danish prisoners in Germany. Before my departure I had submitted my plans not only to the Swedish Government, but also to the President of the Red Cross, Prince Charles. He had expressed the opinion that the scheme must embrace Danes as well as Norwegians. Consequently the field of operations had widened.

BERLIN

February, 1945.

I had no illusions as to the difficulties of my task, and little hope of obtaining more than a partial success. Though well aware of the many obstacles in my path, I persuaded myself that if I could only meet Himmler I could not fail to obtain some concession. The difficulty was just how to contact this man, at the time believed to be the most powerful personage in Germany. He commanded the German armies on the Oder Front, and as the Russian pressure on them was very great, his presence on this Front was indispensable. My difficulties were not diminished by the fact that I could not give the real reason for my visit to those whose help I was counting on to bring about a meeting. Any disapproval of my aims, and they would see to it that the meeting never came off.

When I arrived in Berlin the Yalta Conference had just ended according to the communiqué issued by Churchill, Roosevelt and Stalin, the Allies were now going to co-ordinate their forces and launch a simultaneous attack on Germany from East, West, North and South. The Russians had already advanced well into the Reich, and in the West the British and Americans were beginning their great Rhine offensive. But though the Reich was commencing to crumble, the terror went on in the occupied territories. Between February 8th and 10th no less than thirty-four patriots had been murdered by the Germans in Norway. Events were rushing with increasing speed to the final crisis when anything might happen.

Berlin looked war-weary. The people looked fairly well fed, and though there were long queues outside food shops, in the end customers apparently got what they wanted. There was no real shortage of food, but people gave the impression of being utterly sick of the war and completely dominated by the wish to see it end quickly. The erection of barricades in the streets had begun. There was no panic, but neither was there any enthusiasm. The citizens of the Third Reich worked with the mechanical sense of duty which is characteristic of the German. The men mostly belonged to the Volkssturm, but there were women as well, and a good many foreign workers from the concentration camps. On closer inspection the barricades looked very flimsy.

Anything which happened to be handy was used; 'buses, tramcars and cars were placed in position and filled with bricks and rubble. If the work proceeded without much enthusiasm, the Berliners had not lost their caustic sense of humour. One of the jokes of that time was that when the Russians came to Berlin it would take them one hour and two minutes to capture each barricade. One hour for Homeric laughter, and the remaining two minutes to overcome the barricade.

At the barricades and in food queues the Berliners waited for the enemy's arrival, and around them, in all directions, death and destruction increased day by day. In the central parts of the city four houses out of every five appeared to have been destroyed by the terrific bombardments. Many of the inhabitants had, of course, been evacuated, but most of them remained, living in cellars, and if things were not actually at their best, life still went on fairly normally. The underground railways, as well as gas, electricity and telephones, ceased functioning during air-raids.

One wondered what the people thought of the general situation; what thoughts were hidden behind their dull, apathetic faces. It is certain, however, that their faith in the Nazi system had been severely shaken, and that despite Doctor Goebbels's 'pep talks', the belief was general that Germany had lost the war. Very characteristically there was often an inability, or perhaps I should say, disinclination, to realize that the blame for the whole disaster rested with Hitler. A large part of the population clung sentimentally to their Führer right up to the end. They felt their oath of allegiance binding upon them. Adolf Hitler's fantastic dreams, which to other nations were nightmares, had become to the Germans wishful thinking. They could not bear to lose their faith in him, who had appeared to them as a Redeemer, and in the Nazi system.

The Chief of the Security Police, Obergruppenführer Kaltenbrunner, was courteous though as he offered me Chesterfield cigarettes and Dubonnet – doubtless looted in France – but the eyes which he fixed on me were cold and enquiring. The meeting which had been arranged by the Swedish Legation was at Kaltenbrunner's luxurious home at Wannsee, on the day following my arrival in Berlin. My immediate object was to convince Kaltenbrunner, Himmler's second-in-command in the Gestapo, that it was essential for me to meet his Chief.

Obergruppenführer Kaltenbrunner could look back with pride upon a distinguished career, and he had earned the well-merited confidence of his superiors. He had always shown zeal and efficiency, and had quickly risen to be Chief of the Gestapo in Vienna. When the notorious Heydrich, appointed Protector of Bohemia and Moravia, was murdered, after having himself murdered an unknown number of Czech patriots, Kaltenbrunner was the obvious successor as Head of the Gestapo. Not only had nature provided him with the necessary qualifications, but in appearance he was all that one would expect a Gestapo chief to be. It was fairly obvious that Obergruppenführer Kaltenbrunner could have little understanding for any humanitarian action in connection with the German concentration camps.

At our meeting he showed himself courteous, cold and, as I have said, wary. He was anxious to know why I wished to see Himmler. As he sipped his Dubonnet, he pointed out how extremely difficult it was to arrange a meeting. He suggested that instead I should explain my objects to him, when he would transmit them to his chief. This, of course, was quite unacceptable to me. It was,

Heinrich Himmler

Obergruppenführer Kaltenbrunner

therefore, necessary to get him sufficiently interested to arrange a meeting with Himmler, without giving away the real object of my visit. According to my notes our conversation was roughly the following:

Bernadotte: As you are doubtless aware, relations between Sweden and Germany are extremely bad. Swedish public opinion is intensely anti-German. This is principally due to German cruelty in Norway and Denmark, the taking of hostages, and the scorched earth policy in Northern Norway. German methods in these countries are often in flagrant violation of international conventions. Reichsminister Himmler occupies a position which would make it possible for him to adopt measures calculated to improve Swedish-German relations. As I understand the situation, this would be principally in Germany's interests.

Kaltenbrunner: Are you acting under official instructions?

Bernadotte: No, but I can assure you that what I have told you corresponds with the feelings and wishes of the Swedish people as well as with those of the Government.

Kaltenbrunner: I am well aware that the relations between our two countries are most unsatisfactory, and I deplore it. I also know that Reichminister Himmler is particularly anxious to bring about good relations between Germany and Sweden. But I must point out that the taking of hostages has proved necessary in the fight against sabotage. Similar measures have been taken by the Russians without Swedish public opinion roused.

Bernadotte: It appears to me that it should be of great importance for Germany not to make an enemy of Sweden, whether Germany wins the war or not.

At this point the third person present at the meeting joined in the conversation. It was Brigadeführer Schellenberg. He remarked: 'It would be a great misfortune for Germany if Sweden were to be dragged into the war against her.'

As Brigadeführer Schellenberg was to play so important a part in my future activities, a few words about him would not be out of place.

Walter Schellenberg, a man of about thirty-five, gave me the impression of being the antithesis of Kaltenbrunner. He was a lawyer by profession, and in 1940 was appointed Head of the Political Section of the German Intelligence Service and in 1944 Head of the whole organization. In this capacity he played a very important part, especially as he, from what I gathered, had energetically worked to bring about a change in the policy of the Third Reich, especially in its foreign policy. He had, moreover, tried to combat the bestialities of the Gestapo. During my long confidential talks with him he told me that Kaltenbrunner hated him, and had even, though without success, tried to make Himmler believe that he was in the pay of the British Secret Service. I am quite willing to admit that from the first I felt a certain confidence in Schellenberg, and in any case I shall always be grateful to him for the valuable help he gave me in connection with my Red Cross work in Germany.

The discussion went on and Kaltenbrunner did his best to pump me about my proposals to Himmler, and asked if I had any concrete suggestions. I said that I had not, and generally tried to avoid going too deeply into matters with Kaltenbrunner, for if he were to disapprove of my objectives, he could easily wreck my hopes of meeting his chief. I told him, however, that there were principally two concessions I wanted. One was the issue of exit permits for Swedish women married to Germans, and for their children, particularly for those whose homes had been bombed, or whose husbands were killed or missing. The other was permission for the Swedish Red Cross to work in the Internment Camps in Germany. Oddly enough, Kaltenbrunner showed himself reasonable and understanding on these points, and I asked him if he now saw how important it was that I should see Himmler personally, even though a favourable reply to these requests would not be enough to bring about a change in Swedish public opinion. Kaltenbrunner assured me emphatically that he quite agreed. When I left him I felt that I had made good progress, and had reason to be hopeful about my chances of a talk with Himmler.

The Minister for Foreign Affairs of the Reich, Joachim von Ribbentrop, received me at the Foreign Office. This building had been bombed, though the rooms where I was received appeared undamaged. Ribbentrop seemed to be in excellent form, and filled with the consciousness of his own importance and dignity. He invited me to be seated by the fire, and immediately began to talk. I surreptitiously started my stop-watch.

I should mention here that only a few hours after my arrival in Berlin it was reported to me that the Foreign Office was displaying the greatest interest in my visit, and was especially anxious to know the reasons for my wishing to meet Himmler. It was no secret that the relations between Herr von Ribbentrop and the Head of the Gestapo were decidedly cool. While I was dining in the temporary quarters of the Swedish Legation in the Rauchstrasse – quite close to the old Legation which had been completely destroyed in a recent air-raid – a message from Ribbentrop had reached me, expressing the wish to see me at the Foreign Office the following day. In consequence I motored straight there from Obergruppenführer Kaltenbrunner's residence.

I stopped my stop-watch. It told me that the Minister for Foreign Affairs had talked for one hour and seven minutes without my being given an opportunity to get in a word. Again quoting from my notes, this is fairly exactly the tenor of his talk.

After having expressed, in the warmest and most flattering terms, his great appreciation of my contribution to the exchange of Prisoners of War, and the work of the Swedish Red Cross in Holland and elsewhere, he threw himself into what I can only describe as an oration. It was delivered in tones which at times trembled with emotion, at others resembled a roar, suitable only to the tribune of a packed Kroll Opera House. In between these extremes, he commented on his own personal achievements with simulated humility. He began his address by explaining to me the differences between National Socialism and Bolshevism. In his view Hitler had succeeded in convincing the German working-man of the necessity of retaining the classes that make up society, though these had to be adapted to the Nazi ideology. Bolshevism, on the other hand, had taught that the privileged classes must be 'liquidated'. This, in Ribbentrop's opinion, was the fundamental difference between the two systems. He thereupon proceeded to explain why it had been an absolute necessity for Germany to conclude a pact with the Soviet Union in 1939, and spoke of certain conversations that had taken place between him, Stalin and Molotov. The reason why Ribbentrop had invited the Commissar for Foreign Affairs to Berlin was the growing suspicion of Russia, and the desire to know exactly what her attitude was. One of the reasons for this suspicion was the fact that, on the occasion of certain trade negotiations, the Soviet had sent no fewer than nine hundred and sixty delegates. It was clear that the Russians had come for the purpose of spying out the land. Everything showed that war between Germany and Russia was inevitable, and reliable evidence had actually been received that it was Russia's intention to attack Germany in August, 1941 But what had made any further hesitation impossible was a conversation which Ribbentrop had had with Molotov during an air-raid which began after a State Banquet in honour of the Russian Commissar for Foreign Affairs. On this occasion they had been obliged to spend several hours in a shelter, and Molotov had made use of the occasion to insist on Germany guaranteeing Russia certain bases on the Skagerak and the Kattegat, a demand which Ribbentrop refused with equal firmness, as he had no wish to see the Scandinavian countries exposed to the danger of Bolshevization. Should the German Eastern Front collapse, the whole of Europe was in grave danger of becoming Bolshevized, Ribbentrop went on. He asserted that he knew all the details of Stalin's plans for Europe, which aimed at nothing less than the creation of a number of Soviet Republics in Europe. He went so far as to tell me the names of the individuals Stalin had chosen to be the leaders of these satellites of the Soviet Union. However, he diplomatically left out his own country and Scandinavia. He assured me that if Germany were to lose the war, Russian bombers would be over Stockholm within six months, and that the Bolsheviks would shoot all the members of the Royal Family, myself included. From talks he had had with Stalin, he was also convinced that it was his intention to subjugate, not only the whole of Europe, but also India and China, and that, therefore, every bomb Churchill and Roosevelt dropped on Germany was another nail in the coffins of the British Empire and the USA. He told me that he was at that very time making a last attempt, through special channels, to convince the Governments of the Anglo-Saxon countries of the fate that awaited Europe if Germany were to collapse, and he was going to appeal to Churchill and Roosevelt to stop the offensive in the West, and the aerial bombardments. He added that he had very little hope of success.

After that Ribbentrop appeared to me to contradict himself. Summing up, he concluded that it would be more advantageous to Germany if Russia occupied the European Continent, rather than the Western Allies. He went on to say that if the German High Command should decide that the Oder Line could no longer be held, they would prefer to 'throw themselves in the arms of Russia' and transfer a number of divisions to the West, rather than surrender to England and America. If the Oder Line cracked, it was a sign that Fate had decided that Europe should be Bolshevized. That would, he maintained, happen in any case, even though Western and Central Germany be occupied by British and American armies, for Stalin would, after a short period, insist on their being replaced by Russians.

Subsequent talks I had with a number of leading Germans confirmed that Ribbentrop belonged to the school of German statesmen who advocated an arrangement with the Soviet Union. He was in favour of a strong Russia, and an equally powerful Germany, dominating Europe. Many of the Germans with whom I spoke expressed the fear that this school would gain the ascendancy. When this subject was discussed I always maintained, that even if such be the case, Stalin would never agree to a coalition which would automatically end his country's alliance with Britain and America.

Ribbentrop continued the subject by saying that Hitler was the only one who had realized that the Continent would become Bolshevized if Germany collapsed. It was an appalling tragedy that Britain and Germany should have gone to war against each other, the more so, as this war could so easily have been prevented if Britain had not attacked Germany. He also deplored the blindness of the Finnish Government in making a separate peace with Russia, and predicted that Marshal Mannerheim would soon share the fate of the Rumanian and Bulgarian leaders. In other words, he would be shot.

Speaking of the occupied countries, he said he was convinced that Germany had made a mistake in dealing too gently with the population of these countries. Here he turned to address a question to me. Who, he asked, did I regard as the contemporary being who had contributed most to humanity. Without giving me time to reply he answered his own question. 'Adolf Hitler. Unquestionably Adolf Hitler.' Adolf Hitler was, said the Reichsminister, filled with the friendliest feelings for Sweden. And there was no one living, he added, whom he venerated as much as Sweden's monarch. Here at last I was able to get a word in. Just as I had said to Kaltenbrunner, I told Ribbentrop of the very hostile feelings against Germany among the Swedish people, but this only gave Ribbentrop an opportunity to air his own, rather original, ideas. He said that this Swedish hostility was deplored in Germany, but he, personally, was quite unable to understand it. He thought it a great advantage to Sweden that there were German troops in Norway, for if there were not, the English would certainly have occupied that country, and they would not have shown the respect for Sweden's frontiers that Germany had shown.

Before I left, Ribbentrop asked me if I had any concrete proposals calculated to improve the relations between the two countries, to which I replied that I hoped the Swedish Red Cross would be allowed to carry out certain work in the concentration camps, and that this would make a favourable impression in Sweden. I had no intention of letting him know my real objects. Ribbentrop approved of my scheme and said he was glad I was going to meet Himmler. I suggested that we should have another talk after that meeting, and this was agreed upon.

Someone once called Herr von Ribbentrop the Bismarck of the Twentieth Century. And it is unquestionably a fact that, in his way, he has continued the work of the Iron Chancellor, but it is equally true that in the end he contributed enormously to its destruction. Nor can it be denied that he has stamped the foreign policy of the Third

Reich with his own personality since that day, in 1938, when he was installed in the Wilhelmstrasse. He triumphed in Munich in 1938 and the following year in Prague. But his greatest triumph was in Moscow, in 1939, when he put his signature on the Germano–Russian pact. And now, in the Spring of 1945, when I talked to him and a number of other Nazi bigwigs, I had the impression that he still had Hitler's ear and enjoyed his support. Ribbentrop was the man who had shown the World what Germany was able to do in the field of foreign policy. It was evident that in Hitler's eyes, Ribbentrop was a man who had earned the gratitude of his country.

Sitting with him in his room in the Auswartiges Amt and listening to his long-winded speech, which reminded me of a somewhat worn gramophone record, I reflected that here was a man of very small mental stature, and, moreover, rather ridiculous. It was an astonishing thought, that this man had all these years been Minister for Foreign Affairs of the German Reich. But there was no doubt that he now realized that the game was lost, though he occasionally assured one that the very opposite was the case. He believed that he had the solution to the problems that were piling up higher

and higher in the path of Germany and himself.
He would repeat his famous coup of 1939 when he
made the pact with Russia. He would find a new
road to Moscow. It was plain to me that this was in
his mind when I left him that February night to go
to my car, which was waiting for me in the
Wilhelmstrasse.

My hopes were not to be disappointed. My
request for a meeting with Himmler had been
granted, and at 5 p.m. on February 12th I was
fetched by Schellenberg and driven with him to
Hohen-Luchen, a large hospital seventy-five miles
from Berlin in a northerly direction., The Head
Physician, Professor Gebhardt, himself down with
pneumonia, received me in his sickroom and gave
me some details of his establishment. It was filled
to the last bed, he said. Among these German
refugees, he said, there were numerous children,
and about eighty of them had had to have
amputations because of frostbite and bullet
wounds. It was a grim picture the Professor
presented to me, and it was against this background that I was to meet Heinrich Himmler,
Supreme Head of the SS, the Gestapo, the whole
German Police System, Minister of the Interior

and Commander-in-Chief of the Home Army, the man who by means of his terror system had stained politics with crime in a manner hitherto unknown, and who, by means of this very system, had up to now held the tottering Third Reich upright.

In his *Berlin Diary* William Shirer describes Himmler as a quiet little man who looks like a harmless country schoolmaster. I entirely agree with this as an excellent superficial description of the Gestapo Chief. When I suddenly saw him before me in the green Waffen SS uniform, without any decorations and wearing horn-rimmed spectacles, he looked a typical unimportant official, and one would certainly have passed him in the street without noticing him. He had small, well-shaped, delicate hands, which were carefully manicured, although this was forbidden in the SS. He was to my great surprise extremely affable. He was humorous and amusing, and frequently made use of a joke when conversation was threatening to become awkward or heavy. Certainly there was nothing diabolical in his appearance. Nor did I observe any sign of that icy hardness in his look, of which I had heard so much.

In his talks with me I found Himmler a very vivacious personality, inclined to sentimentality where his relations with the Führer were concerned, and with a great capacity for enthusiasm.

It was an amazing experience to hear this man who had sent millions of human beings to their death by the most shameful methods, speak with enthusiasm of the chivalrous manner in which the English and the Germans waged war in France in the summer of 1944, when actions had on occasion been interrupted in order that the wounded could be collected.

A Norwegian who had worked among Norwegian prisoners of war in Germany had told me that Himmler took a deep interest in Scandinavian Runic inscriptions, and at the end of our talk I presented him with a Swedish seventeenth-century work on this subject. Himmler seemed quite affected by this, and told me that he was deeply touched by and grateful for my thought in giving him this pleasure under present conditions. He had at one time used his influence on behalf of Professor Seip, Rector of the University of Oslo and one of the most heroic figures among the Norwegian patriots. Was this due to apprehension regarding the fate he knew awaited him, or was it admiration for a man who did not fear to speak his mind fearlessly? Whatever the explanation of this may be, Himmler was certainly one of the most contradictory characters I have ever encountered. The experiences of Professor Seip, and Bishop Berggrav, another great Norwegian patriot, which they related to me, correspond with my own observations and impressions. Himmler ordered Professor Seip to be released from the concentration camp where he had been incarcerated, and, apologizing for the brutal manner in which he had been treated, offered him every facility for continuing his scientific studies in Germany, with the same remuneration he had received as Rector of the University of Oslo. Seip told me that he regarded Himmler as a kind of idealist, with a particular liking for the Scandinavian countries. And when I met Bishop Berggrav in Oslo, in the middle of May this year, he expressed a similar view. He told me that one day Himmler had visited him. Berggrav asked him if he wanted him to talk frankly, or to say the kind of things Himmler would like to hear. Himmler told him he would be very interested to hear his honest opinion. After this talk Terboven had demanded Berggrav's execution, which was vetoed by Himmler.

Nothing can, however, exonerate Heinrich Himmler from the terrible guilt which rests on his shoulders, no excuse can ever be found for his conduct. It was he who created the concentration camp system, and even if, as he asserted, he was unaware of the horrible cruelties to which this system gave rise, it is he who must bear the responsibility. When I talked to him he indicated in various ways that he well knew this to be the case. He also showed that he was fully conscious of the immense difficulty of the situation in which he found himself. These difficulties were partly connected with the military position, and partly with his relations towards his Führer, Adolf Hitler.

Every German would fight like a lion before he gave up hope, Himmler declared, when I asked him if he didn't think it meaningless to go on with the war, as Germany could not possibly be victorious. Certainly the military situation was grave, very grave, but not hopeless. When he took over the command of the Oder Front there was a breach of 220 miles in the line which invited a penetration by the Russians. He had orders to close this breach, and he succeeded in calling up fresh levies and even bringing up troops from less exposed Fronts. There was no immediate risk of a Russian break through on the Oder Front, Himmler declared.

It was probably the 'inner front' which was Himmler's greatest headache. It was evident that at that period he was still in close contact with Hitler. In any case he made this plain himself, emphasizing his unswerving devotion to his Führer. 'You may think it sentimental, even absurd, but I have sworn loyalty to Adolf Hitler, and as a soldier and as a German I cannot go back on my oath. Because of this I cannot do anything in opposition to the Führer's plans and wishes.'

It is almost certain that Hitler was in full power at that time. To some extent the actual leadership may have passed out of his hands, but it was easy to see that many of those nearest to him continued to have great respect for him and did not dare to oppose him. His influence was still considerable, although it was gradually acquiring a more and more negative character. He no longer initiated new measures, he merely vetoed those of his collaborators.

Shortly before my arrival in Germany the former President of the Swiss Federal Republic, Musy, had come to an agreement with Himmler which provided for the Jews interned in the concentration camp at Theresienstadt to be transported to Switzerland, *en route* for USA. The foreign press got wind of this and published the facts. This was reported to Hitler by one of his press observers, and Himmler was summoned to appear before the Führer. Asked by the latter what concessions Germany had obtained in exchange, Himmler replied that Germany had obtained nothing at all, whereupon Hitler was seized by one of his attacks of rage and forbade any further transportations of this kind. Himmler had to accept this decision, the transportations ceased, and when Musy returned to Berlin he found it impossible to arrange a meeting with the Head of the Gestapo.

It was with this background that I began my work in Germany. Hitler raging because of the concession made, and Himmler not daring, or unable to oppose his master. Schellenberg told me that at this period a certain strain in the relations between the Führer and the Head of the Gestapo was noticeable. Himmler declared his unswerving loyalty. But his freedom of action was restricted.

'Is it your intention that the Norwegians and Danes now in German concentration camps, which you want sent to Sweden, shall there be given Police training? Do you really regard this as the conduct of a neutral country?' Himmler shot this at me sharply, and when I replied that I had nothing to do with these matters, he immediately went on: 'If I were to agree to your proposals the Swedish papers would announce with big headlines that the war-criminal Himmler, in terror of punishment for his crimes, was trying to buy his freedom.'

We had now reached the crucial point in our talk, which lasted two hours and a half, and at which Schellenberg was present. As was my practice, I had begun by pointing out the hostile feeling to Germany in Sweden, whereupon Himmler at once counter-attacked and produced a number of arguments to illustrate the innocence and humanity of Germany's policy. The bad feeling was, he said, entirely the fault of the agitation of the Swedish press, in particular *Göteborgs Handelstidning*. It was the Allies who had begun the system of dropping saboteurs by parachute. It was since the Allied occupation, and not during the German occupation, that conditions had deteriorated to a catastrophic degree in France, Holland, Belgium and Greece. It would have been a simple affair for the Germans to have occupied the whole of France in 1941, but they refrained from doing so. It was absolutely essential to act forcefully, in fact with the greatest ruthlessness, in communities where the population had begun to fight the German troops openly.

Himmler offered excuses, justifications and explanations for everything, but he also made an admission. When I asked him if he himself would not take up arms against the invader, if he were a citizen of an occupied country, and if he did not think the Norwegian Freedom Fighters were performing a patriotic and national duty, he replied in the affirmative. But, he hastened to add, saboteurs must be prepared to take the consequences of their acts. I answered by saying that it was not this which had roused such indignation in Sweden, but the method of taking hostages, and the killing of so many innocent people, which was contrary to humanitarian and international conceptions. Himmler denied that this had taken place, whereupon I gave him a few definite cases. He said there could be no question but that I was misinformed. At a subsequent meeting he himself brought up a case I had mentioned, and admitted that an enquiry he had instituted showed that my facts were correct. If this was a premeditated piece of acting, it was certainly well done. Then came the usual question. Had I any concrete proposals?

I asked him if it would not be better if he were to suggest any measures which could improve the situation, to which he replied that he could suggest nothing. It was at this point that I made the proposal about the release of Norwegians and Danes for internment in Sweden, to which Himmler reacted so violently. In addition to what has already been mentioned, he said that Sweden and the Allies in any case must give some compensation for such a concession, as, for example, an assurance that sabotage would cease in Norway.

One felt the shadow of Hitler over us at that moment. After the agreement with Musy, Hitler had at once asked what concession Germany had obtained. If Himmler came to terms with me, the same question would be hurled at him. It was evident that Himmler's hands were tied, that he was not so powerful as many believed. The Führer was alive, and whatever the reason, he could not be ignored.

I told Himmler that the concession he had mentioned was out of the question.

I had met with an uncompromising refusal, but the bargaining was not over. I changed the course of our conversation and said that the Swedish Red Cross was very anxious to obtain permission to work in the concentration camps, especially in those where Norwegians and Danes were interned.

Himmler: This would probably be very useful, and I see no reason why permission to do this should not be granted.

Bernadotte: And to facilitate the work, the Norwegians and Danes in question should be collected into two camps, one for each group. The total number of Norwegian and Danish prisoners is probably somewhere about thirteen thousand.

Himmler: That figure is greatly exaggerated. I don't know the exact number, but I should not think it can be more than two or three thousand. However, I will look into the matter.

Himmler had accepted my proposal. He also agreed that the aged, the sick, and mothers should be allowed to return to Norway after having been assembled in the camps. He did not even raise any objection to the Swedish Red Cross staff being admitted to the camps to assist in the collecting of the prisoners.

There remained one subject, a delicate as well as an important one. It concerned Swedish women who had married Germans and were, in consequence, German citizens, and these we were determined to get out of Germany. When I raised the subject, I emphasized that I quite understood the German standpoint, that it was the duty of all

German citizens to take their share of the burden imposed by the existing situation, but pointed out how desirable it was that these women who had lost their homes, or whose husbands and grown-up sons were either killed or missing, should be removed to Sweden where they could be looked after by their relatives. The Swedish Legation had prepared lists of these people, and I now handed Himmler several which only contained the most distressing cases. His face clouded over when he discovered that the list included a number of children.

'I don't feel inclined to send German children to Sweden,' he said. 'There they will be brought up to hate their country, and spat at by their playmates, because their fathers were German.' When I tried to calm him down, and pointed out that it should be a comforting thought to German fathers to know that their children were in safety in Sweden, he retorted: 'Their fathers would no doubt much rather see them grow up in a shack in Germany than have them given refuge in a castle in a country which is so hostile to Germany as Sweden is.'

In spite of this he gave the lists to Schellenberg, who later told me that I could look upon the matter as settled. He said he would himself see to it that there was no hitch.

After this, our conversation became more general, and the Head of the Gestapo led it on to the Bolshevik danger, much on the same lines as Ribbentrop. He predicted that the end of Europe would come if the German Eastern Front were to break down, for the Second World War was a war between Europeans and Asiatics. There would be no future for Europe if the Allies were victorious. Only in the last weeks more than a hundred thousand German women varying in age from sixteen to eighty had been violated by the Russian hordes – he simply could not understand Sweden's blindness in the face of the immense danger from the East.

Bernadotte: But Germany was allied to Russia during part of this war. How does that fit in with what you have just said?

Himmler: I thought you would say that. We made a mistake, but we soon realized that the Russian armed might was so great that it was only a matter of time before it would be turned against us.

In the course of this visit to Germany I obtained fairly reliable evidence that Himmler had during the whole war been opposed to an attack on Sweden. His opponent here had always been Herr von Ribbentrop, who had favoured this policy.

While we sat there talking about past events and conditions, the Front for which he was responsible, and which was situated at no great distance from us, was beginning to crack, just as Germany was beginning to crack, and everyone knew that the end was not far off. He returned to the subject of Sweden, and said: 'It is with the deepest gratitude and admiration that we Germans recollect Sweden's humanitarian acts during the First World War. During this war we have not seen much evidence of this, but we have nevertheless a certain regard for Sweden. As an example, I can mention the fact that we did not bother to occupy you in 1941. It would have been a simple matter then.'

Bernadotte: That may be true, but it would not be quite so simple now.

Himmler: As a matter of fact we never even thought of occupying either Sweden or Switzerland, in spite of what your press alleges. Speaking of your press, I can tell you I had decided that no Norwegian students were to be sent to Germany, but when I heard of the menacing tone of the Swedish papers, and their threats, I at once gave orders for the removal of the students to Germany.

Bernadotte: The Swedish press showed itself critical of the Allies, too. For instance, after the

Crimean Conference, and because of certain people being placed on the Black List.

Himmler: I can't say I have noticed that. As for the Black List, I suppose I head the list.

I explained that the Black List was not a list of War Criminals, but concerned commercial matters. Himmler laughed and said that in that case it did not concern him.

In the beginning of this century a boy was growing up in South Germany whose name was to become known throughout the world. He came of a simple middle-class family, and his father had been tutor to one of the Princes of the Bavarian Royal House. During the First World War the boy enlisted in the Bavarian Guards and advanced to the rank of Sergeant-Major at the age of sixteen. When the war ended he returned home and joined the National Socialist Movement at its very beginning.

'Those were glorious days,' said Himmler – he had been talking of his own life. 'We members of the movement were in constant danger of our lives, but we were not afraid. Adolf Hitler led us and held us together. They were the most wonderful years of my life. Then I could fight for what I regarded as Germany's re-birth.' He ended by saying that, after all, the movement had contributed real benefits, particularly in respect to Social Legislation. As I listened to him my thoughts went to the millions of Jews who had been murdered while 'the Movement' was in power. And I was also during this conversation struck by the incongruity of the Supreme Commander of the German Home Army in the last phase of the World War never having had a higher military education than that of Sergeant-Major.

While we were talking about various matters I asked him if he would not admit that there were decent people among the Jews, just as there were among all races, and told him that I had many Jewish friends. To my surprise he admitted I was right, but added that we in Sweden had no Jewish problem and could therefore not understand the German point of view. An indication that Himmler had of late changed his attitude towards the Jews could probably be found in his agreement with Musy. Later on Himmler, on my suggestion, agreed that if the necessity should arise, he would have interned Jews handed over to the Allied military authorities instead of removing them from the concentration camps where they were held.

Before leaving, I returned to the subject of the Scandinavian prisoners being collected in two camps, and said it was evident that our ideas as to the numbers involved varied very greatly. I therefore asked for confirmation that the persons liberated should include civilians in the concentration camps. Himmler gave me this assurance, and promised to let me have definite answers to the matters we had discussed before I returned to Sweden. When I said good-bye to him he turned to Schellenberg and asked him if he had chosen a good chauffeur for me. Schellenberg replied that he had got the best man he could as the journey to Berlin was rather dangerous on account of the many tank traps and barricades that had been put upon the roads. 'Good,' said Himmler, 'otherwise it might happen that the Swedish papers would come out with big headlines announcing: "WAR CRIMINAL HIMMLER MURDERS COUNT BERNADOTTE".' With these words he left the room.

Herr von Ribbentrop was affable and helpful. When I called on him at the Foreign Office on Wednesday, February 21st, to tell him, as agreed, the results of my talk with Himmler, he raised no difficulties. He had already been informed of the subjects discussed with Himmler through a memorandum, and told me that he would not oppose the assembling of the Norwegian and Danish prisoners, in two camps, and that Swedish-born women would be given exit visas for Sweden. He pointed out, however, that the German authorities could not undertake to arrange transportation, as all vehicles were required for the war. The Swedish Red Cross must provide its own transport, as well as fuel. Herr von Ribbentrop seemed pleased when I told him that this could easily be arranged, and that I would accompany the column. He promised to support me with Himmler and to assist me in every way. Then he returned to his favourite subject. Referring to the latest developments in the situation, principally the bombing of Dresden and Nürnberg and their consequences, he asserted that there was a growing inclination among the Nazis towards Communism. I then said good-bye to Herr von Ribbentrop and left.

Himmler kept his word and let me have a definite decision before I left for home. Immediately after my visit to the Minister for Foreign Affairs I lunched with Brigadeführer Schellenberg, who told me that Himmler had several times talked to him about my visit, which had pleased him. Schellenberg was authorized to inform me that Himmler had definitely given his consent to the proposals which I had submitted to him; Swedish-born women were to receive exit visas, with the reservation that if any of them had had any trouble with the Police, the case should be submitted to him personally for examination, and the Norwegian and Danish prisoners were to be assembled in a camp at Neuengamme, situated not far from Hamburg. I was further given permission to establish contact with Professor Seip (as a matter of fact I had already done so) who had been liberated, and now represented Norwegian interests in Germany as well as with the Danish Legation in Berlin. On my side I promised to endeavour to have my Red Cross Column ready at Warnemünde ten days later.

STOCKHOLM – BERLIN – FRIEDRICHSRUH

Stockholm, *March*, 1945.

It was with an easier mind that I returned to Stockholm. The foundations had been laid, it should be possible to save many lives, and Sweden would be able to be of real help to her Scandinavian neighbours. On my return I immediately reported to my Government, who approved my arrangements with Himmler and von Ribbentrop, and also agreed to my suggestion that a Red Cross detachment be despatched at the expense of the State, the equipment and material to be supplied by the military authorities. I also reported to the Commander-in-Chief, General Jung, who also gave his approval to the plan. The work of organizing the expedition was immediately begun by the General Staff of Defence and the General Staff of the Army.

As the German authorities had stipulated that the number of personnel must not exceed two hundred and fifty, the detachment was arranged as follows: three platoons each of twelve road coaches and one platoon of twelve lorries. The detachment further included mobile field kitchens, workshops, ambulances and a quarter-master's platoon. Colonel Gottfrid Björck was appointed leader of the expedition. All the personnel were volunteers chosen from regulars and conscripts in the armed forces. The military designations on their uniforms were replaced by those of the Red Cross. After the detachment had been assembled in

Skåne,* it was despatched by boat to Denmark via Malmö, and on March 11th found itself in Odense where the Danish Red Cross had arranged billeting and meals, and the Municipality and townspeople showed us magnificent hospitality. Everything was done by the Danish authorities to facilitate our journey.

On March 12th we crossed the German frontier. Our route was planned to go via Flemsburg, Kiel, Lübeck, to castle Friedrichsruh, which was to be our Headquarters. We reached our destination late at night on the same day, and were welcomed by the owners of the castle, Prince and Princess Otto von Bismarck, who during our whole stay did everything to facilitate our task in a practical way, as well as by great hospitality and kindness.

A telephone message from Berlin: Obergruppenführer Kaltenbrunner was on the warpath. And other people in Himmler's immediate entourage as well. This information came from the most reliable source, from Brigadeführer Schellenberg, who had very intimate contact with the Swedish Legation in Berlin. Kaltenbrunner was endeavouring to wreck my arrangement with

* The Swedish province facing Denmark.

Himmler. He had on several occasions said to the Danish representatives in Berlin that I must be very innocent if I imagined that Swedish Red Cross delegates would be allowed access to the German concentration camps, and that it was unthinkable that Danish and Norwegian prisoners would be allowed to be transported to Sweden.

Kaltenbrunner's reasoning was not difficult to follow. Not only did the Swedish plan appear to him wholly unnecessary, but it was intolerable from the point of view of the Third Reich. Neutral representatives would, if this were permitted, obtain far too intimate a view of conditions in the various camps, the long and carefully preserved secret of their horrors would be revealed, and the last remains of Nazi prestige vanish. When I spoke to the Swedish Legation, from whom the telephone message came, I replied sharply that I would not tolerate my arrangement with Himmler being interfered with by any subordinate, and that I declined to discuss these matters with anyone but Himmler personally. The decisions taken could only be revoked by a new agreement between Himmler and myself. I said this, well aware that our telephone conversation was being tapped and would soon reach Kaltenbrunner's ears.

This episode gives an interesting side-light on the conditions prevailing during the last grim act of the Nazi drama. One could hear the death rattle, dissolution had already commenced, but the intrigues among the hierarchy were as bitter as ever. I know that Schellenberg played an active and valuable part in these days which were so critical for our mission, and I do not believe that it would have been brought to a successful conclusion if it had not been for his powerful support. He told me later that Himmler had said that the promise he had given me must not be broken. Himmler himself, later, gave me an account of what he had experienced during this time, when he had been compelled to overcome very strong opposition to get the scheme carried through. He added, sadly, that the order and efficiency which his subordinates had displayed formerly had gravely deteriorated as a result of Germany's precarious military situation. And meanwhile the Allies' Front was getting closer and closer to Germany's heart.

It became clear to me that I must return to Berlin. On March 5th I flew to Berlin where I at once began negotiations with Schellenberg, as well as with his antagonist, Kaltenbrunner. The Head of the Security Police now came into the open as my opponent.

Kaltenbrunner: I do not intend to assist you in this matter you have brought up.

Bernadotte: And I am not going to stand one of Himmler's subordinates trying to sabotage an arrangement agreed upon between him and myself.

The gloves were off. The fight had begun.

Half a century earlier the political world had its eyes sharply focused on Schloss Friedrichsruh, for it was to Friedrichsruh that the old Chancellor, Otto von Bismarck, had withdrawn after his forced resignation in March, 1890. It was from here that he carried on his campaign against the 'new course' of German policy. It was here that he wrote his highly critical articles about William II and also his famous *Gedanken und Erinnerungen.* It was at Friedrichsruh that he received the homage of the German People, here vast numbers came as on a pilgrimage to demonstrate their love for the aged statesman. And it was here that he ended his days.

Now Friedrichsruh had become the Headquarters of a Swedish errand of mercy at the final stage of the Second World War. Soon the old Castle was to find itself in the very front line of the war.

On March 9th I went to Friedrichsruh to await the arrival of the Red Cross detachment. Our work during March included three large transports to Neunburg i.e., two thousand two hundred Danes and Norwegians from the concentration camp at Sachsenhausen, situated North of Berlin, six hundred Scandinavians from Dachau, North of Munich, and sixteen hundred policemen from various camps situated North-west of Dresden. The transportations from Sachsenhausen were carried out in seven relays, between March 15th and March 30th. As soon as we had made sure of a supply of fuel a column of thirty-five vehicles was formed for the run to Dachau, a distance there and back of eleven hundred miles. The column left on March 19th, under the command of Colonel Björck personally, and by March 24th the task had been completed without any mishaps. At the end of March the Danish policemen had been collected from the various camps.

It is not necessary for me to enter into a detailed account of the work of the expedition, as I understand that this will be the subject of a special report.

Another Bismarck estate was to play a part in the events of those days, Schönhausen, one hundred and twenty-five miles West of Berlin. It was on this family estate that the Iron Chancellor was born and brought up, and no doubt also absorbed the Junker ideals to which he remained faithful throughout his life. Now the Swedish Legation had been installed at Schönhausen, and during my work in Berlin we motored to the capital from the old manor almost every morning. These drives gave one a pretty clear picture of conditions in Germany two months before the surrender. All main roads were barricaded, and one could see men of the Volkstürm as well as prisoners of war working on the barricades. All cars, and, for that matter, all travellers on the roads, were subjected to most careful control. I had, however, been provided with a pass by the Ministry of Police, which enabled me to proceed unhindered.

On the occasion of my first drive from Schönhausen to Berlin I saw for the first time women prisoners from concentration camps. There were hundreds of them, foreign women as well as Germans who were suspected of having worked against the Nazi régime, guarded by male and female warders as they marched wearily to their work. It was a dreadful sight. A painful sight, too, were the long lines of refugees from East Prussia. When we passed these unfortunates weeks

Count Bernadotte's car outside Schönhausen

Count Bernadotte taking cover during an air-raid

must have lapsed since they had abandoned their homes. They were being directed to different centres where the local authorities would be responsible for their billeting and feeding. They appeared worn and weary, and utterly hopeless. There was no future for them, and the present was an inferno. Whatever they had possessed was lost, material goods as well as any belief in life. Silently the pitiable procession moved on, along roads lined with the carcases of emaciated horses who had drawn the primitive vehicles until their strength gave out. These vehicles were similar to the 'covered wagons' used by the early settlers in America. The tarpaulin or similar covering with which they had been hastily covered was the only protection available for the women and children at night, and I was told that earlier in the year thousands of refugees had frozen to death. The winter had been very severe in Silesia and East Prussia.

Travel in those days was chaotic. The only way was by car as trains took an incredible time to get from one place to another. But motoring was not free from excitement, for German fighter planes and German Ack-Ack had almost ceased to exist during the last months of the war, and Allied airmen were able to attack all vehicles on the roads without interference. My car was painted white and bore the Red Cross flag as well as a Swedish flag, but this was not of much help. The Allied authorities had announced in Stockholm that because of the intensification of the air war, immunity for the Swedish Red Cross vehicles could not be guaranteed.

I recollect one day, at the end of March, when I was on my way from Schönhausen to Friedrichsruh. We had just passed the small town of Perleberg, half way between Berlin and Hamburg, when we heard the sound of explosions. It was an Allied air-raid on Perleberg. We continued on our way when, after a while, we saw six American bombers approaching us at a low altitude. My chauffeur and I jumped out of the car and took cover behind some trees. A moment later the bombers swept over us at a height of only about thirty feet. I readily admit that I felt cold shivers down my spine, but our luck held out. The Americans attacked an objective a few hundred yards from where we were and then disappeared.

But my most exciting drive came a little later. On April 20th I left Friedrichsruh to go to Berlin, where I had a meeting with Himmler. The war in the air had by then become so intensified that I was advised to take special precautions. I took two chauffeurs, one of whom, seated on the travelling trunk at the back of the car, was to act as observer. He was instructed to signal by banging the top of the car as soon as he saw Allied planes approaching, to warn us to stop, jump out and take whatever cover we could find. On our way we passed through the town of Nauen, twenty-six miles to the West of the capital. We noticed blue and yellow flags, a signal that an air-raid was on, but as nothing seemed to be happening we continued on our way until we reached the outskirts of the town. Seeing an old woman by the side of the road we pulled up, and I asked her if a raid was on. Before she had time to reply, we heard the dull drone of a large number of Allied bombers. A few seconds later bombs were dropped on the railway station, less than a hundred yards away. We drove on out of the town and took cover in a trench which had been dug at the side of the road for the defence of the adjoining village, the plan apparently being to sweep the road with anti-tank guns.

There was brilliant sunshine and a cloudless sky as the Allied bombers swooped on towards their targets. For about an hour we lay in our trench, gazing at the fascinating spectacle which presented itself to our eyes as Nauen and neighbouring villages were heavily attacked. We could see the bombs leaving the planes, after which what looked like a white column of smoke rushed towards the ground at great speed and then a terrifying explosion. This was the first time I observed anything approaching panic among the German population. A crowded shelter had been hit, a number of people killed, and men and women came running across the fields, aimlessly seeking shelter in ditches and anything that offered cover of any kind. It was as if the people of Nauen felt that nothing could save them, since not even a few fighters from the near-by airfield of Spandau came up to engage the enemy.

A few days later in Denmark I had another proof of the paralysis which had seized the Luftwaffe. A Danish ambulance had been placed at my disposal, and we were just about to take off from a German airfield at Skustrup in Southern Jutland when the air-raid warning was sounded, and we saw American fighters attacking some military installations nearby. We hastily got out of our plane and found the American fighters coming towards us at a great speed. We threw ourselves into a trench and almost at the same moment nine fighters roared over our heads, their machine-guns firing for all they were worth. The attack lasted for several hours, and when it was over I sought out the German Commander and asked him why he had not ordered some of his own machines to go up, for I had seen them, well camouflaged, on the outlying parts of the airfield. He shrugged his shoulders and replied: 'Oh, I have got the machines all right, but not a drop of petrol, so they are of no use to me at all.'

German troops were retreating, on the roads near Hamburg, at Neu-Brandenburg and near other towns. Small disorderly groups, almost without arms, almost as hopeless as the refugees from the East, soldiers who realized that the war was lost, that this was the end. I noticed groups of them, almost a platoon in strength, unarmed but for a couple of rifles. When I pointed this out to representatives of the military authorities, they said, resignedly, that such was unfortunately the case. Arms were coming to an end. The few that remained had to be husbanded. When men were relieved they had to hand over their arms to those who took over. And this was the army which a few years before, in 1940–1941, so nearly conquered all Europe.

As soon as I saw that the work of the Swedish Red Cross detachment had started, I left for Denmark to report to the Danish authorities about our negotiations and the work that we had set in motion. Just before my arrival in Copenhagen the Shell Building had been bombed. This building was the Headquarters of the Gestapo in Denmark, and since they naturally anticipated an attack sooner or later, a typical measure to prevent it being carried out was adopted. A number of Danish Freedom Fighters had been placed in cells on the top floor. The Allies had, however, decided that the building must nevertheless be bombed.

When I arrived in Copenhagen there was great excitement and jubilation because of the highly successful bombing raid. The majority of the imprisoned Freedom Fighters had, as if by a miracle, escaped death, while the voluminous archives of the Gestapo had been destroyed by fire. Unhappily a number of children in a school adjoining the Shell Building had lost their lives.

My audience with King Christian affected me greatly. I had learned enough to realize that he was as important to-day to the Freedom Movement as he had ever been. To the Danish people he was the focal point of their resistance, the Supreme Head of the Freedom Movement. Now, sitting in his invalid chair – he had not yet recovered from injuries sustained in a riding accident some years ago – he was moved to tears as he listened to my account. He expressed his great joy at the results we had so far achieved, and I assured him that we would not stop until we had reached the goal we had set ourselves, till all Danes and Norwegians in the concentration camps had been brought over to Sweden.

I returned to Sweden and arrived in Stockholm on March 22nd.

NEUENGAMME – HOHEN-LUCHEN

March 28th–April 9th, 1945.

We were quite close to the German coast when we received a radio report that a heavy daylight attack on Berlin was in progress. We were able to observe a number of planes in the distance. As it was impossible to distinguish if they were Allied or German planes, our pilot decided to make a landing at Stralsund. We were circling over the airfield when another message reported 'all clear', so we continued on our way and soon reached the German capital, which resembled a sea of flames. A pall of thick smoke covered all the surrounding country, and when Richert, our Minister, met me at the Tempelhof airfield, he told me the 'all clear' had only gone half an hour before.

It was my anxiety lest the activities of the Swedish Red Cross should have a set-back that had led me to return to Germany after only a few days' absence. My experiences had told me how very unstable the situation was. Anything might happen, and if it did, I at least wanted to be on the spot.

And so it was. In Berlin I was informed that our people had not yet been allowed to begin their work at Neuengamme. The German authorities had raised difficulties, and said that the camp must be prepared before we could do anything. According to the agreement, part of Neuengamme was to be set aside for the Scandinavian prisoners, and there was evidently no desire to admit any foreigners until things had been 'tidied up'. Norwegian prisoners informed me later that sanitary measures had been begun in the camps a few weeks before, and that conditions had considerably improved in the section where the

Scandinavians were to be placed. I have, therefore, good reason to believe that the hideous conditions at a later date revealed in, for example, Buchenwald, had existed in Neuengamme too.

It was on Good Friday, March 30th, that I was given the first opportunity to visit Neuengamme concentration camp, where several thousand Scandinavian prisoners had already been assembled by the Swedish Red Cross.

By now the Third Reich was not merely crumbling; it was about to collapse. In the West the British and the Americans had already crossed the Rhine and were advancing on Osnabrück. In the East the Russians were pressing forward and were to enter the suburbs of Vienna a few days later, simultaneously with the sensational Allied advance towards Bremen–Verden. On April 10th Konigsberg and Vienna were taken by the Russians. The goal was Berlin.

We drove up to the entrance of Neuengamme, where the gates were opened for us and closed as soon as we were inside. I was the first representative of a neutral humanitarian organization to visit a concentration camp, for when our people had fetched prisoners in the different camps, they were not allowed to enter; instead, the prisoners were assembled outside the gates where the motor coaches and ambulances were waiting. It was with feelings of great emotion that I prepared to see these revolting creations of the Third Reich, which had aroused such feelings of horror and fear throughout the whole world. Neuengamme was not a bad test case, for it was believed to be one of the worst, quite on a par with Dachau, near Munich, notorious since the first seizure of power by the Nazis.

The Commandant, Obersturmbannführer Pauli, received us in his green SS uniform, looking very smart and military and efficient, an expert in his own line. He had been in Poland, and had at Lublin given incontrovertible proof that he understood how to keep prisoners in concentration camps in order. As a matter of fact he had the reputation of being one of the very worst representatives of his 'profession'. However, he showed himself most courteous to me, and was helpful and reasonable, and agreed to almost everything I proposed. The guns were roaring near Bremen, the Front was approaching nearer and nearer to Berlin, and the Obersturmbannführer probably realized that his professional days were soon to come to an end.

While in America I had met Odd Nansen, the brilliant young architect son of the famous explorer Fridtjof Nansen, and we worked together there until 1940 and became great friends. When he was brought before me and I saw him snatch off his cap and stand to attention as all prisoners were required to do when in the presence of a German of rank, and the Commandant was with me, I boiled with anger at this example of German so-called discipline. Odd Nansen was one of those Norwegians who had risked everything, one of the many sent to concentration camps. Here they were, then, all these Scandinavian patriots, of whom we had been able to obtain a complete list. For in our negotiations with the Germans, some time back, it had been agreed that every prisoner collected by the Swedish detachment should be given a form on which to enter his name and the state of his health. At first the Germans had objected, but I understand that we outmanoeuvred them by pointing out that we would be responsible for the prisoners in our charge getting to Neuengamme, and that we could not accept this responsibility without a list of names. We were thus very quickly in possession of complete statistics concerning all the Scandinavian prisoners at Neuengamme, and able to transmit them forthwith to the Danish and Norwegian authorities and organizations concerned.

I well remember the first hutments I inspected. The Commandant, who accompanied me everywhere, made no objections when I wanted to speak to the prisoners, and even agreed to my speaking Swedish with them, though I thought it wiser not to carry on long conversations in that language, in order not to make him suspicious. In this particular building were lodged the Danish policemen who had been sent to Germany when the German authorities in Denmark suppressed the police. Some of these men had been at Neuengamme before, after which they had been moved to other camps, and had shown little enthusiasm when told they were going back to this camp where their experiences had been the worst possible. And when I looked round I could well understand their feelings. The discipline was evidently barbarous and the overcrowding appalling. In most of the huts wooden pallets had been laid on the floor, and these, covered with sacks, made up the prisoners' beds. What the conditions would be, were an epidemic to break out, could be imagined. Among the prisoners were Norwegian and Danish doctors who had done all they could to help their comrades. Assisted by them, we at once set about improving conditions. The Swedish Red Cross had obtained permission to send a number of delegates to work inside the camps, and under the leadership of Professor Rundberg they, without delay, began to improve the sanitary conditions. Odd Nansen, who had already drawn up a plan showing how the hospital barrack should be reconstructed, was of splendid assistance. We also arranged for medicines and portable buildings to be sent to Neuengamme from Denmark.

One episode during this visit remains in my memory. We had arranged to hold a conference in one of the hospital barracks at which were present not only delegates of the camp staff, but also, invited by me, the Danish and Norwegian doctors, as well as representatives chosen by the other prisoners. Something tremendous had entered into the existence of these men, for it was certainly the first time they had been invited to take part in a discussion, seated at a conference table. It was touching to see how their spirits rose, how their faces lit up, how hope was reborn, when I was able to tell them that in a few days they would be sent back to Denmark.

When I departed from the camp, the Danes and Norwegians had gathered along the electrified wire enclosure which surrounded the camp. I called to them 'Paagjensyn',* and saw the happiness of their eyes, and hoped that they really understood that we had no intention of leaving before accomplishing the task we had set ourselves. But I thought, too, of the prisoners of whom I had caught a glimpse in a part of the camp where there were no Scandinavians, and where we had no power. There were thousands of unhappy human beings there, or rather human wrecks, wandering aimlessly about the camp, apathetic, vacant-minded, incapable of ever returning to a normal existence.

The military situation was now developing at such a pace that it was clear that Neuengamme would shortly be in the zone of operations, and I had a serious talk with the Commandant about the position. I told him that if it became necessary to evacuate the camp, he must see that the Danes and Norwegians were sent North, either to Northern Schleswig or to Denmark. The great advantage gained by having them all assembled in one camp near the Danish frontier must not be lost.

* 'Au revoir' in Danish.

Obersturmbannführer Pauli promised to see that my wish was carried out, whereupon I left for Berlin to have my second meeting with Himmler.

The meeting was on April 2nd. As before, I visited Himmler at the Sanatorium of Hohen-Luchen administered by Professor Gebhardt, whose friendship with Himmler went back to their school-days. When the SS Leader entered the room I noticed that he was not only grave, but nervy, and during our talk, which went on for four hours, he did not attempt to deny that he regarded the situation as most critical, though he would not admit that it was hopeless. It was during this long conversation that my activities in Germany were to be given a new direction. I suddenly realized that I had been dragged into the vortex of high politics.

Himmler: I am ready to do anything for the German Nation, but the war must go on. I have given my oath to the Führer, and that oath is a binding one.

Bernadotte: Don't you realize that Germany has lost the war? By attacking Russia in 1941 you yourselves made it a war on two fronts, and it was that which snatched victory from your grasp. You yourself say that you are willing to do anything for the German Nation, and if that is true you ought to think more of them than of your loyalty to Hitler, if you consider his decision to continue the war a disaster for your country, involving the death of tens of thousands more on the military front as well as on the interior front. A person in your position, bearing such an enormous responsibility, cannot obey a superior blindly, but must have the courage to accept responsibility for decisions which are in the interest of the people.

Himmler did not answer. A few moments later he was called to the telephone and rose quickly and left the room. Brigadeführer Schellenberg, who was again present at our talk, turned to me and asked me if I could not see Eisenhower to discuss with him the possibilities of arranging a capitulation on the Western Front. I told him that this was quite impossible, that the initiative must come from Himmler, and that I was unwilling to act as intermediary, since this might be taken to indicate that I believed that Eisenhower and the Western Allies would be willing to negotiate for an armistice. I said I was convinced that this was not the case.

Himmler returned and we began to discuss the Danish–Norwegian transportations, and the camp at Neuengamme. I told him that the transportations had, on the whole, been successful, but that conditions in the camp, which I had inspected, were more than wretched. Again I asked, especially in view of the fact that at that time tens of thousands of German refugees were being sent to Denmark, that all Danish and Norwegian prisoners should be allowed to be sent to Sweden. Himmler answered that personally he would grant my request with pleasure, but that he could not possibly do so. One felt the hand of Hitler. Hitler was against this, and Himmler did not dare to oppose him. At this point, however, Himmler began to compromise. 'A way would be,' he said, 'to let some of the prisoners leave now – if all were to be sent at the same time it would attract too much attention.' I submitted a scheme which was at once accepted, that all Swedish and Norwegian women, and all invalids, should be despatched to Sweden, as well as a small proportion of the four hundred and sixty-one Norwegian students in Neuengamme. The actual number could be decided later. All the Danish policemen were to be sent to Denmark. The Scandinavians sent to Sweden were not to be interned, but placed in hospitals or boarded out. They would, however, be required to give an undertaking not to return to Norway or Denmark, or to go to England, but to remain in Sweden till the war was over. Subject to the same condition, Himmler further agreed to a certain number of interned Norwegian civilians, among them Professor Seip, and some French citizens, being set free.

I had made progress, and the situation looked more hopeful from my point of view, but Himmler was filled with gloom.

Himmler: The German Government has made fatal mistakes. It was a mistake not to be more frank with England. As for me – well, of course, I am regarded as the cruellest and most sadistic man alive. But one thing I want to put on record: I have never publicly vilified Germany's enemies.

Bernadotte: If you haven't, Hitler has done so all the more thoroughly. What was it he said? 'We shall erase all English cities.' Is it, then, so surprising that the Allies have bombed German towns systematically?

Himmler replied to this by asserting that bombing was not started by the Germans, but I reminded him of Warsaw, in 1939, and Rotterdam, in 1940. He received this in silence, and shortly afterwards rose with the remark that he had to discuss certain routine matters with Schellenberg. The audience was over.

Schellenberg accompanied me to Berlin, and talked the whole way in a confidential but rather forced manner. What he related gave me a good picture of what was happening behind the German political scene. He told me that after leaving me, Himmler had continued the topic of a capitulation in the West, and but for Hitler would not have hesitated to ask me to go to Eisenhower. However, he had hinted, the situation might alter; Hitler's position might be weakened, it might happen any moment . . .

Himmler had asked Schellenberg to convey to me the message that if this should happen, he hoped I would immediately proceed to Allied Headquarters. Continuing, Schellenberg said that Himmler was in a very difficult position, torn between his desire to save Germany from utter chaos and his loyalty to the Führer. Finally he uttered a warning. He warned me that Obergruppenführer Kaltenbrunner, Chief of the Security Police, and possessing great influence over Hitler, was furious about the concessions Himmler had granted me, and that Kaltenbrunner was a very dangerous man. Himmler had, therefore, told Schellenberg to caution me not to speak of the matters we had discussed on the telephone, as Kaltenbrunner had given orders that all telephones I might use should be carefully tapped.

During the following days I had several more talks with Schellenberg, who had had further conferences with Himmler. He thought the latter, together with other leading figures in the Nazi hierarchy, would soon leave for South Germany. I advised Schellenberg in such an event to remain in North Germany and to obtain from Himmler wide powers, especially as regards the Scandinavian prisoners of war, so that in such a situation they could be removed to Sweden. He promised to do his best to arrange this, and informed me that Himmler had once more returned to the question of my going to Eisenhower. I now told Schellenberg in plain words what my attitude in the matter was, and that he must rid his mind of any illusions that the Allies would ever enter into negotiations with Himmler. The latter could only conceivably head the government during a short period of transition, after which it would be taken over by the Allied occupation authorities. It was, however, I said, possible that Himmler might in this way prevent Germany being plunged into complete chaos.

I then proceeded to specify my conditions. I said I was prepared to go to Eisenhower's Headquarters on the following conditions:

1. There must be an announcement from Himmler that Hitler – compelled by illness to give up his powers – had chosen him to be the leader of the German People.
2. Himmler must declare the National Socialist Party dissolved, and remove all Party officials.
3. Himmler must order the activity of the so-called 'Werewolves' to cease.
4. Before my departure I must have confirmation from Friedrichsruh that orders had been given for the despatch to Sweden of all Danish and Norwegian prisoners.

The acceptance and carrying out of these conditions meant a revolution in Germany. They meant that Himmler would depose Hitler, dissolve the National Socialist Party and put an end to the Third Reich. Personally I never imagined Himmler would accept these conditions, but Schellenberg did not hesitate. He told me that he would try to induce his chief to accept them.

On this occasion Schellenberg also gave me the

information that Hitler had given orders that the concentration camps at Buchenwald, Bergen-Belsen and probably also Theresienstadt should be evacuated, and the prisoners compelled to cover a distance of about one hundred and ninety miles on foot. Schellenberg said he had protested strongly against this, and that after a stormy discussion he had succeeded in inducing Hitler to countermand the order. The Commandants of the camps had been instructed not to evacuate them, but to surrender the prisoners to the Allied troops. Similar instructions would be given in connection with Neuengamme.

Corruption was rife in Germany. With a packet of cigarettes, half a litre of spirits, or a small quantity of coffee, one could do pretty well anything. I had good evidence of this when I got out of my car at Tempelhof. I was accompanied by Professor Seip and his wife, who had joined her husband in captivity. Himmler had given his consent to their leaving the country, but their papers had not come through in time, and the authorities had informed us that they could leave in spite of this. We had some exciting moments at Tempelhof airfield, waiting to see how the local officials would act. A packet of cigarettes did the trick, and Professor Seip and his wife were allowed to go on board the plane. Soon after we took off, and I don't think that on all my travels in Germany I had felt such real happiness as I did then.

That was on April 9th – five years to a day after the German invasion of Norway.

FRIEDRICHSRUH BERLIN – HOHEN-LUCHEN – FLENSBURG – LÜBECK

April 19th–April 24th, 1945.

Ten days later, General Patton had penetrated into Czechoslovakia. Northern Holland was liberated, resistance in Hamburg had been crushed, and in Berlin the defence was staggering before the Russian assault. Hitler issued the order: 'Shoot any officers who order retreat.'

When I climbed into the night train from Stockholm to Malmö, on April 18th, I knew great events were imminent, but I had no idea that they would be as sensational as proved to be the case. On my arrival in Copenhagen on the morning of the 19th, I was flown to an airfield in Sonderjylland

and was met by a delegate of the Swedish Red Cross at the Danish–German frontier. The report he made to me was very alarming. It appeared that a couple of days earlier the Danish Consul-General in Hamburg had been in contact with Reichstadthalter Kauffman with whom he had arranged for the Scandinavian prisoners who had been assembled at Neuengamme to be sent to Denmark immediately. When the German 'Party Representative' in Hamburg heard about this, he at once got in touch with Himmler, who evidently knew nothing about the arrangement, and gave orders that no transportations of any kind should take place. He also stopped the transfer of sick Scandinavians which had gone on for some time between Neuengamme and Sweden.

The atmosphere at Friedrichsruh was gloomy when I arrived there, and it did not cheer me up when the German liaison officer informed me that in his opinion the chance of getting the transfers continued was very small. However, the same evening he looked me up after dinner and told me that the whole camp at Neuengamme was to be evacuated immediately and the prisoners transported to Denmark. Afterwards I heard the explanation of this sudden change from Himmler himself. The reason for the evacuation of the entire camp of Neuengamme was the publicity which the Allies had given to the conditions in the concentration camps at Buchenwald and Bergen-Belsen, which he, however, declared to be a tissue of lies. I replied that, in my opinion, the persons who had reported about these conditions were so trustworthy that one could not doubt the truth of their accounts. Himmler completely went off the deep end and gave me the following version of what had occurred. It appeared that one of the Allies' tanks for some reason burst into flames when it approached one of the camps, and the Allied officers, thinking this was caused by firing of the German guards, ordered fire to be opened on the camp, with the result that one of the buildings had been set on fire. This, said Himmler, was the explanation of the many charred bodies found when the Allies entered the camp. 'It is disgusting,' the Head of the Gestapo added, 'that this camp which in my opinion was in the best condition, should have become the object of these shameful descriptions. Nothing has upset me so much as what the press of the Allies has said in this connection.'

The next day we started removing all Scandinavians from Neuengamme. The success with which this task was carried out was not least due to the extraordinarily great assistance we received from the Danish Jutland corps, which had been organized with most commendable speed, and arrived at Neuengamme only twelve hours later. The Scandinavians were saved, but what became of all the other prisoners who numbered about twenty thousand? I don't know, and I was not present when the evacuation was carried out, but my Swedish comrades told me that it was hurried and brutal. The non-Scandinavians were pushed into goods trains whose destination no one knew. Questioned about this the German Commandant shrugged his shoulders: 'keine Ahnung' (I have no idea). The goods trains, like others of those ghostly trains which had in the last years so often steamed eastward in German-occupied countries, disappeared in the distance with their human cargo and had not been heard of since.

April 20th – Adolf Hitler's birthday. Doctor Goebbels announced: 'Our Führer has not deserted us. This is our victory.' Two days later the Russian troops began to penetrate into Berlin.

It gave me a strange feeling to arrive in Berlin on this day, which in other years had been celebrated with such enthusiasm by the Führer's faithful, devoted, admiring people. Now Berlin had become a silent city, the barricades were completed, and people wandered about waiting for what was going to happen.

An air-raid warning compelled me to spend several hours in the shelter of the Swedish Legation, after which I immediately sought out Brigadeführer Schellenberg who informed me that Himmler was not to be found in Berlin. I pointed out that it was essential for me to return to Friedrichsruh the following morning and asked him to do his utmost to arrange a meeting some time during the night of April 20th–21st. A few hours passed and then came a message from Schellenberg asking me to proceed to Hohen-Luchen Sanatorium, where I would be able to see Himmler in the course of the night. When I left Berlin in the afternoon, I could hear the thunder of the Russian guns.

The roads were crowded with troops and with refugees, and progress was not easy. However, we got to our destination by nine o'clock the same evening, and I was informed by Professor Gebhardt that he had not yet heard from Himmler. There was nothing to do but to wait. We dined, and I was shown over the hospital which was filled with wounded soldiers from the Eastern Front, and even invited to be present when some were operated on. At half past twelve at night there was a telephone message that Himmler would arrive at Hohen-Luchen for breakfast at 6 a.m.

The Head of the Gestapo was a very tired and weary man when he entered the breakfast-room at the appointed hour. Perhaps he felt he must give some explanation, for he told me that he had hardly slept a wink for several nights. One felt that he was unable to remain long in one spot, and travelled from place to place to get an outlet for his anxiety and restlessness.

The breakfast was ample and excellent, and Himmler ate with a good appetite. Occasionally he tapped his front teeth with his finger nail, which, according to Schellenberg, was a sure sign that he was in a nervy state. This time our talk was entirely about humanitarian measures, and I again put forward the request that the Scandinavian prisoners, who were at the time being transported to Denmark, should be allowed to continue the journey to Sweden, but Himmler once more refused. Schellenberg subsequently told me that Hitler had again forbidden any concession on this point.

Himmler, however, agreed to some of my other requests. He agreed that if Denmark should become a battleground, the Scandinavian prisoners of war were to be transported to Sweden through the help of the Swedish Red Cross. He also showed genuine interest in my proposal that the Swedish Red Cross be allowed to fetch all French women interned at Ravensbruck concentration camp, and said that he not only agreed to this, but that he wished us to remove women of all nationalities from these, as the camp in question was shortly to be evacuated. I promised him that I would immediately give our detachment orders to this effect.

'The military situation is grave, very grave,' Himmler remarked, but he showed no inclination to continue the subject.

I departed for Friedrichsruh immediately after breakfast. After a short visit to our Headquarters where I made arrangements for the removal of the women interned at Ravensbruck, I left for Denmark, to be more exact, for the small town of Padborg, just north of the Danish–German frontier. There I had the opportunity of inspecting the excellent arrangements made by the Danish Red Cross, and the Danish authorities, for the reception and quartering of prisoners before they were removed to other places in Denmark. Here, too, I saw for the first time the well-known Froslev camp, situated near Padborg. Because of the transportations from Germany which we had carried out in the last few days, the camp was very crowded, but spirits were high among the Danish and Norwegian prisoners. It is true that they were still being guarded by the Gestapo, that they were still under German orders, but the mere fact of having left Germany behind them made their hearts lighter. And certainly the Danish food was very different from what they had been given in Germany. 'Du gamla, du fria . . .' (Thou ancient and free). These men and women who had risked their lives for their country stood there softly humming or whistling under their breath the Swedish national song. It was when I stepped out on to the steps of the hospital hut that I had this experience, which was perhaps the most moving of all. It was a salute that went straight to my heart. These people were still captives, though they felt freedom was within reach. But they well knew what would happen if at that moment German camp-discipline were to be enforced. They risked that, desiring to show their gratitude, and they could not have done so in a more moving manner.

At 3 a.m. the following morning I was awakened by the telephone. It was the Chief of the Flensburg Gestapo, who informed me that Brigadeführer Schellenberg wished to speak to me about a most urgent matter. As I had promised to visit another camp in Jutland which had been prepared for Scandinavian prisoners of war arriving from Germany, I was only able to go to Flensburg later in the day, and met Schellenberg there at 3 p.m.

That was on April 23rd. Schellenberg lost no time in letting off his bombshell. Hitler was finished. It was thought that he could not live more than a couple of days at the outside.

That same day. Dr. Goebbels had announced that the Führer had arrived in Berlin where he would in person lead the defence.

Schellenberg continued his report of the situation.

Schellenberg: Himmler has decided to bring about a meeting with General Eisenhower to inform him that he is willing to give orders to the German forces in the West to capitulate. Would you be prepared to take this message to General Eisenhower?

Bernadotte: It would be better if Himmler's wishes were transmitted to the Swedish Government, who could then, if they were willing, transmit them to the representatives of the Western

Powers. But in no circumstances will I forward such a communiqué to the Swedish Minister for Foreign Affairs, Günther, unless Himmler promises that the German forces in Norway and Denmark shall capitulate too. In any case it is most doubtful if the Western Allies will agree to capitulation on the Western Front alone. But even if such should be the case, there is no necessity for a personal meeting between Himmler and Eisenhower. Himmler need only order the German General in command to lay down his arms. And, as I have pointed out before, there is no question of Himmler playing any part in the Germany of the future. At most, the Allies might want to use his services for the carrying of the surrender.

Schellenberg declared that he quite understood my points of view and said that he would endeavour to make them clear to Himmler before the latter and I met again. He got on to Himmler on the telephone, and it was arranged that we should meet in Lübeck that night, the night of April 23rd–24th.

I shall not easily forget that night with its uncanny feeling of disaster. Himmler arrived at the local branch of the Swedish Legation about half an hour before midnight. Immediately after the sirens went, and I asked Himmler if he wished to go down to the shelter, adding that I could not promise that we should be left undisturbed, as one could, naturally, not prevent other inhabitants of the building, or passers-by, from taking cover. He hesitated a moment, and then decided to go down. A small group of Swedes and Germans had already collected in the shelter, and Himmler talked to the Germans, clearly trying to find out what popular feeling was. It was quite obvious that he was not recognized. During the hour we spent in the shelter I looked curiously at him from time to time. He struck me as being utterly exhausted and in a very nervy state, and looked as if he were exerting all his will-power to preserve an appearance of outward calm.

Again the sirens shrieked – 'all clear'. We left the shelter and sat down in one of the rooms of the Legation and proceeded to discuss the subjects about which Himmler had come to consult with me. It was now about half an hour after midnight, and as the electricity was not working, a couple of candles on our 'conference table' were the only illumination.

The Head of the Gestapo began his review of the situation by saying that it was quite possible that

Hitler was already dead, and if he were not, he would certainly be so within the next few days. The Führer had gone to Berlin to die with the inhabitants of the capital. Berlin was surrounded, and it was only a question of a few days, Himmler said, before it would fall. On the three previous occasions when we had met I had suggested to him that he should end the war. He said that he had recognized that I was right, that the situation was hopeless, that the war must end and Germany admit herself defeated, but he had not been able to break his oath to the Führer. Now matters were different. It was quite possible that Hitler was already dead . . .

'I admit that Germany is beaten.' The Head of the Gestapo uttered these words with a resigned gesture. What was going to happen? Himmler, continuing this line of thought, took up a subject of decisive importance to Europe, to the future of the whole world. In his own manner he touched on the importance of the creation of a Hitler legend, which one may very soon see launched, and which after the fall of the Third Reich will play the same part as the 'stab in the back' after the Peace of Versailles. Everything would depend, said Himmler, on how the Allies treated Germany. If the Allied Nations had the intention of crushing the German People, then Hitler would come to be regarded as the greatest of their heroes. It would be said that not only had Adolf Hitler been able to solve their internal problems, he had also raised them out of the 'state of degradation' in which they had found themselves after the Peace of Versailles, in order, in the end, to die the death of a hero at the head of his People, on the barricades of Berlin.

If I may be permitted to diverge for a moment, I must say here that all I have experienced and learnt has firmly convinced me that the myth that Hitler died fighting on the barricades of his capital must be destroyed once and for all, and as soon as possible. Adolf Hitler was, in the Spring of 1945, a psychologically and physically sick man. A heroic act was the last thing of which he was capable. His decision to stay in Berlin was almost certainly due to his knowledge that, whatever happened, only a short time remained for him to live. For the German People, especially, it is of particular importance that this fact be made quite clear: there is nothing of the hero in the manner of Adolf Hitler's death. The accounts of his last heroic fight are a pure myth. He died like a hunted man, and as a cowardly man, as cowardly as all his henchmen showed themselves in the days of the break-up. The most fatal thing which could happen would be that the German People should feel themselves impelled to place Adolf Hitler on a pedestal.

The conference went on.

Himmler: In the situation which has now arisen, I consider my hands free. In order to save as great a part of Germany as possible from a Russian invasion I am willing to capitulate on the Western Front to enable the Western Allies to advance rapidly towards the East. But I am not prepared to capitulate on the Eastern Front. I have always been, and I shall always remain, a sworn enemy of Bolshevism. In the beginning of the world war I fought tooth and nail against the Russo–German pact. Are you willing to forward a communiqué on these lines to the Swedish Minister for Foreign Affairs, so that he can inform the Western Powers of my proposal?

Bernadotte: It is in my opinion quite impossible to carry out a surrender on the Western Front and to continue fighting on the Eastern Front. It can be looked upon as quite certain that England and America will not make any separate settlements with Germany.

Himmler: I am well aware how extremely difficult this is, but all the same I want to make the attempt to save millions of Germans from a Russian occupation.

Bernadotte: I am not willing to forward your communiqué to the Swedish Minister for Foreign Affairs, unless you promise that Denmark and Norway shall be included in the surrender.

Himmler replied without hesitation that he agreed to this, and had no objections to make against American, British or Swedish troops occupying Denmark and Norway, when the German troops would lay down their arms. He made only one reservation: Denmark or Norway should not be occupied by Russian troops. I asked Himmler what he proposed to do if he received a negative reply to his offer. He replied: 'In such a case I shall take over the command on the Eastern Front and be killed in battle.'

As is known, he did not carry out his intention.

After having again pointed out that I was extremely doubtful regarding the chances of the Western Powers agreeing to his proposal, I asked him to write a short letter to the Swedish Minister for Foreign Affairs, Günther, which I would hand to him as ocular evidence that Himmler really desired to make the necessary contact through me. Himmler immediately did as requested. He also declared that if a meeting could be arranged between him and Eisenhower he was willing to make, roughly, the following declaration: 'I recognize that German arms have been defeated by the Western Powers. I am prepared to surrender unconditionally on the Western Front, and also to discuss technical ways and means to carry out the capitulation of the German Armed Forces in Denmark and Norway.'

This Himmler declared was the bitterest day in his life.

It was agreed that I should return to Sweden as quickly as possible, and, through Schellenberg, let Himmler know the result of his move. Before leaving, I touched on two further questions. I told him that the executions in Denmark must cease – he must himself realize that they could only result in an increase in the burning hatred which the Danes felt towards Germany and the Germans. I again referred to the question of the liberation of King Leopold of Belgium. In both cases Himmler promised to grant my wish.

We departed from the Legation. It was about half-past three in the morning. Himmler insisted on driving the car himself, as he was now returning to the Eastern Front. As luck would have it, on starting he immediately ran into the barbed wire which surrounded the building, and we had a hard job to get the car clear. Our Secretary of Legation, Torsten Brandel, and our Attaché, Count Axel Lewenhaupt, who witnessed our departure, agreed with me that there was something symbolical about the manner in which Himmler made his exit.

Later in the morning, I returned with Schellenberg to Flensburg. He told me that Himmler had again spoken about his projected meeting with Eisenhower. He had tried to enter into the spirit of such a meeting, and had asked if Schellenberg thought that he ought to make a bow to the Allied Supreme Commander and if he ought to shake hands.

Later in the morning of the same day I departed by ambulance plane for Copenhagen, and from there continued to Stockholm. At Kastrup the Swedish Minister, Dardel, met me, to whom I reported everything that had occurred, as communications between Stockholm and Schellenberg ought to go via the Swedish Minister in Copenhagen to our Attaché, Lewenhaupt, whom I had asked to remain at Aabenraa.

STOCKHOLM – ODENSE – AABENRAA –
COPENHAGEN

Stockholm, *April 24th–May 7th,* 1945.

On my arrival in Stockholm on April 24th I immediately called at the Foreign Office, where I met His Excellency M. Günther, M. Boheman, the Permanent Under-Secretary of State, and von Post, the Head of the Political Department of the Foreign Office, at nine o'clock. An hour later His Excellency M. Günther and I called on the Prime Minister, and at eleven o'clock we arrived at the Foreign Office, where I made my report. Himmler's proposal was directed exclusively to the Western Allies, a method of negotiation which, according to the officials of the Foreign Office, was not practicable in view of the obvious necessity that the Soviet Union should be informed. However, in order to inform the Allies of Himmler's willingness to negotiate, which was in itself somewhat sensational, a meeting was held later that evening at which were present the British Minister, Sir Victor Mallet, the American Minister, Mr. Herschel Johnson, M. Boheman and myself.

The two foreign diplomats pointed out that it was most unlikely that their Governments would agree to Himmler's proposal, and that they must necessarily confer with the Moscow Government.

Two more days passed. During the evening of April 26th, M. Boheman rang me up to inform me that the American reply, signed by President Truman, had arrived. I at once went to the American Legation, where I found Mr. Johnson and Boheman. The telegram read:

> *A German offer of surrender will only be accepted on condition that it is complete on all fronts as regards Great Britain, the Soviet Union as well as USA. When these conditions have been fulfilled, the German forces must immediately on all fronts lay down their arms to the local Allied Commanders. Should resistance continue anywhere, the Allied attacks will be ruthlessly carried on until complete victory has been gained.*

M. Boheman and I, on leaving the American Legation, went on to the residence of the Minister for Foreign Affairs, who pointed out that the answer from the United States was anything but unexpected. It was decided that I should leave without delay and meet Schellenberg and hand the answer to him. The Foreign Minister said that if I went personally to present the answer, a break in the possibilities of negotiations would be avoided, and that in this way it might be possible to continue the discussions about a German capitulation in Norway and Denmark. On April 27th I flew to Odense, where I met Brigadeführer Schellenberg, to whom I presented the Western Powers' reply to Himmler's offer of capitulation. At first it seemed to make him very depressed. There was now, he said, scarcely any possibility of a solution. After we had discussed the matter for a while he seemed to become more hopeful. In spite of everything, he thought that there might be a way to bring about capitulation in Norway and Denmark, thus preventing these two countries from becoming theatres of war, with its consequent devastation. We arranged to meet the following day in Lübeck in order to continue the discussion with Himmler.

I put up at the house of a Danish official, Amtman Thomsen, in Aabenraa, where Brigade-führer Schellenberg called on me the following morning. He informed me that it was impossible for Himmler to come to Lübeck, as he had departed for a place north of Bremen, and wished us to meet there. Schellenberg and I agreed that there was no point in my proceeding into the actual battle zone, but that he should go alone to acquaint Himmler with the situation.

This was on April 28th. When later in the afternoon I sat listening to the so-called 'Atlantic Sender's' news report, I heard my name mentioned. This was followed by the announcement that according to reports from London and New York I had opened negotiations with the Head of the SS, Reichsminister Himmler, for a German capitulation. My first thought was that this had spoilt everything, and that there was no further possibility of negotiations.

I have since that time rather altered my views about this point. As a matter of fact, the publicity which my negotiations received at this early stage were to be of decisive importance, for they resulted in a very important decision being altered. It appears from everything, that Himmler had from the beginning been chosen to be the Leader of the German Reich. in the event of Hitler's death. The publication of Himmler's offer to surrender, however, altered this. Instead of Himmler, Grand Admiral Dönitz was chosen to be the leader. It is

Brigadeführer Schellenberg

Foreign Minister von Ribbentrop

Admiral Dönitz

Count Schwerin von Krosigk

very doubtful if the Allies could ever have begun negotiations with Himmler because of his terrible reputation. It was far easier with Dönitz. In the first place he belonged to the armed forces, and any action on his part would be received by the Services in quite a different manner to one by Himmler. Also negotiations with him would be less distasteful to the Allies than with the Head of the Gestapo. It appears that Himmler later told Schellenberg that he was very disappointed at having been passed over. On the other hand, he said, he looked upon the situation as so grave that all personal considerations must be sacrificed. He was, therefore, prepared to collaborate loyally with Dönitz. I also believe it to be a fact that Himmler, until the last moment, maintained his conviction that it was absolutely necessary that the German Forces, at least, in Norway and Denmark, should capitulate. In this he was strongly supported not only by Schellenberg but also by the new Minister for Foreign Affairs, Count Schwerin von Krosigk.

Brigadeführer Schellenberg returned from his expedition on April 29th. He had, he told me, found Himmler at a place somewhere north of Bremen, but the meeting had not been a pleasurable one to him. Himmler had got news of the publicity which in England and America had been given to our negotiations, and was furious. At one moment he had threatened to arrest Schellenberg as being the one who, together with myself, had induced him to begin negotiations for surrender. The next moment he had proposed that both he and Schellenberg should place themselves under General Schörner's orders and attack the enemy on the Eastern Front at the head of a battalion. Schellenberg succeeded in calming him down, and after a couple of hours' discussion Himmler declared himself prepared to allow the German troops in Norway to capitulate, and also to allow the Germans in Denmark to lay down their arms to the British forces.

I telephoned to Stockholm at once and requested that a representative of the Foreign Office should immediately proceed to Copenhagen to meet Schellenberg. Having done so, Schellenberg and I departed for Copenhagen by car, and arrived there the same evening.

That day, April 30th, when I took up my negotiations again, Copenhagen was in a state of enormous excitement. There were all kinds of rumours, and the announcement that Germany had capitulated was expected at any moment. My negotiations with Himmler were now general knowledge, and it was believed that I had come to Copenhagen to discuss technical points in connection with the capitulation with Dr. Best, the accredited representative of the Third Reich in Denmark. Enormous crowds had assembled outside the Hotel d'Angleterre on Kongens Nytorv in anticipation of further news.

During a conference at my hotel I heard firing outside in the Square, and when I went to the window I saw thousands of people running in every direction while Hipo-men, who had appeared in their cars, were sweeping the square with tommy-guns. However, the fusillade was not very serious, and I could not see any casualties. But the incident made me understand better than anything before, how great must be the hatred which the Danes felt towards the German invaders, but still more towards those of their countrymen who had entered into the service of the occupying power and become traitors to their own country. These Hipo-men, in their dark blue uniforms, made a vile impression on me. They were young hooligans, who enjoyed the power they still possessed, but which they well knew would soon be taken from them. For me, a member of a neutral nation, this episode was of great value, as it gave me an insight into the suffering of the Danish people during the hard and trying years of the occupation.

After I had conferred with the representative of the Swedish Foreign Office, von Post, and Schellenberg with Dr. Best, and after having given the King of Denmark a brief resumé of the situation, Schellenberg, von Post and I met at the Swedish Legation at 11.30, when Schellenberg reported about his visit to Himmler. The Swedish view was, however, that further elucidation was required, and Schellenberg decided to make another trip to Himmler's headquarters.

Dr. Best was present at the subsequent luncheon at the Legation. It is said – I have heard many Danes say so – that he endeavoured to show himself as humane as possible during the occupation, and that he had several times intervened when the methods of the Gestapo became too brutal. I avoided all questions of high politics, but asked him if he would agree to a number of Englishmen and Americans who had been interned in Denmark since the beginning of the war, being allowed to be transferred to Sweden. He immediately did, and said that he would like this concession to be regarded as a personal favour to me, as he thought that he and his Government owed a debt of gratitude to me for what I had done in connection with the exchange of German and Allied prisoners of war.

May 1st came, and with it, in the evening, the message which millions of people had for years been waiting and longing: Hitler was dead. Grand Admiral Dönitz in his wireless speech announced: 'German men and women, soldiers of the German army, our Führer, Adolf Hitler, has fallen. The German people are bowed in sorrow and reverence . . . The Führer has appointed me to be his successor.' And in an order of the day to the German Army, Dönitz declared: 'The greatest hero in the history of Germany has departed from the scene.'

For me this heroic death meant, so far as I could see, that the points of departure of my negotiations had been shifted. Earlier that day, immediately after my return to Stockholm, I had had a conference with His Excellency, M. Günther, and with M. Boheman, and I then still believed that a solution could be found for the problem of capitulation. Now all these hopes were shattered. It was no longer Himmler who had been placed in the dominating position, but Grand Admiral

Dönitz had instead been chosen to be Hitler's successor. And Dönitz urged the continuation of the battle: 'I take over the supreme command of all branches of the armed forces with the intention of carrying on the war . . .'

The scene, however, changed rapidly. On the evening of May 4th, M. von Post, who had returned to Stockholm on the previous evening, informed me that Schellenberg had returned to Copenhagen. And there Schellenberg had reported some sensational events. In the first place, Grand Admiral Dönitz had decided to surrender with all German forces in Holland, North-west Germany and Denmark. Secondly, Schellenberg was to reach Stockholm the following morning with authority from Dönitz to arrive at an understanding regarding a German surrender in Norway. At ten o'clock in the morning on May 5th Schellenberg, who had been nominated envoy, arrived at Stockholm by special plane, and immediately a meeting took place at my residence between him, M. von Post and myself. Schellenberg presented his credentials, signed by Dönitz, and stated that the new German Minister for Foreign Affairs, Count Schwerin von Krosigk, had asked him to endeavour to arrange a meeting with General Eisenhower for the discussion of a general German surrender.

Schellenberg gave us some other interesting information. In Murwick, in the neighbourhood of Flensburg, he had had a long meeting with Dönitz, Schwerin von Krosigk and Himmler, at which were also present General Field-Marshal Keitel and General Jodl. On this occasion Schellenberg said that he had been able to persuade the Government to order the capitulation of all German troops in Holland, North-west Germany and Denmark. The only one who had violently opposed this was Keitel. M. von Post told Schellenberg that the Swedish Government naturally felt it necessary to inform the representatives of the Allied Powers in Stockholm of what had gone before. Schellenberg expressed the wish that the German Minister, Thomsen, and the representative of the German Military Attaché should leave for the Swedish–Norwegian frontier in order to inform General Böhme of the situation. These two gentlemen took off from Barkarby Airfield at 6.30 p.m. in a Swedish military plane.

The following day, May 6th, Thomsen reported that he had in the morning been met at the frontier by a representative of General Böhme. This officer had informed him that Böhme was unwilling to capitulate with his forces unless he were to receive a direct order from Dönitz. He said that the German forces in Norway were quite intact, and would without difficulty be able to hold out a couple of months longer. He was, therefore, not prepared to act on an order to surrender by Minister Schellenberg.

Immediately afterwards a telephone communication was received from Count Schwerin von Krosigk, who it was reported was at Murwick, together with the other members of the Government. The Minister for Foreign Affairs gave the information that direct contact had been set up between the German Government and General Eisenhower, and that negotiations regarding Norway had been begun. Later in the day Schellenberg succeeded in getting into telephonic communication with Dönitz. He informed the Grand Admiral that apparently General Böhme had not been kept informed of the actual situation, and asked him to transmit a direct order that the capitulation in Norway should be carried out. Dönitz replied that it was possible that he would commence direct negotiations with Eisenhower on this question, and that it was therefore not certain that the Swedish Government's assistance would be needed from then on.

At 10.15 on Monday, May 7th, came the final communication from Count Schwerin von Krosigk. In the night between May 6th and May 7th, said the Minister for Foreign Affairs, Germany's complete capitulation had been decided. Negotiations between him and General Eisenhower about the signing of the capitulation were still proceeding. I at once informed the Crown Prince, General Ehrensvard and M. Boheman of what had happened. I was probably the first Swede to learn of this great event.

This, then, was the end. The war in Europe was behind us. The nightmare which the Nazi system signified had ceased to be a reality. Millions of people could now set their minds on the work of reconstruction, which was to create a happier world. I felt in this moment a very deep gratitude in having been privileged to take a part in the events of the final act, and perhaps thereby to have contributed to bringing about an armistice at an earlier stage than might otherwise have been the case. I had been given an opportunity to follow the events of world history from a close distance. The curtain now descended on a world which had seen a greater degree of evil and suffering than perhaps any earlier period in the history of Europe.

Epilogue

In the course of my travels in Germany, in the spring of 1945, I received much information about the leading figures of the Third Reich from sources which must be regarded as reliable. This information has convinced me that it is extremely important for the future development of the world that absolute clarity be created in two respects.

Firstly, it must be made absolutely clear to the German people that in 1945 Germany suffered a complete defeat, not only on the military front, but on all fronts, just as in 1918, when, however, German propaganda soon produced the 'stab in the back' from the Home Front as the real reason for their defeat. The myth about German invincibility must once and for all be destroyed. No further legends about a 'stab in the back' must be allowed.

Secondly, the German people must be brought to see what kind of men the leaders of the Third Reich were. My experience tells me that they were men lacking in all moral conceptions, in all loftiness of mind. In the last act there they were, with their hideous pasts, desperately intriguing amongst themselves, while at the same time endeavouring to take shelter behind each other's backs, cowardly, undecided, irresolute. The last act of the Third Reich lacked all dignity or majesty. It seemed merely ignominious, because all the *dramatis personae* themselves were ignominious and petty. They were not fighting for an ideal, a belief, a conviction; they were fighting merely for their lives, which had been besmirched by crimes which could never be forgiven.

Let us glance briefly at the leading figures of the Third Reich, as they appeared in its thirteenth and last year. Let us take first the Führer. Already Grand Admiral Dönitz has introduced the legend that the Führer died the death of a hero, fighting for his people on the last barricades of the Occident against Bolshevism. We shall see that in the best-informed German quarters quite a different opinion is held. The Führer did not die like a hero; it can be regarded as quite certain that he was murdered. It is true that he kept his leadership until the very last days of the Third Reich. But he had long before lost all capacity for taking any initiative. All he could do was to veto decisions made by his lieutenants. To his entourage he had become a figure of terror in almost the same degree as he was to the world at large. If anyone displeased him he immediately had an order for execution prepared. At this final stage Adolf Hitler was physically and psychologically a branded man, in all probability marked by that disease which can offer an explanation for his insane acts and ideas. His hands shook, he could no longer walk, he could only cross the room with difficulty. He felt that the sands of his life were running out and was more than conscious of having failed completely, of his enemies being about to corner him, of the situation becoming more and more desperate. Until the last day he would telephone to Himmler, roaring out his accusations in a desperate attempt to conjure up a change in the situation.

In Hitler's closest entourage was, in the first place, Eva Braun, his mistress. Eva Braun, who came from a Munich family, and is said to have been a very beautiful woman, had, I have been told, a very great influence over Hitler. It was, for example, she who paved the way for Obergruppenführer Kaltenbrunner, one of the worst of the evil spirits in the little group of men and women who guided Germany's destiny in those days. Kaltenbrunner was an intimate friend of another member of the set, Gruppenführer Fegelein, who was married to a sister of Eva Braun, and who rapidly advanced from being a humble riding-master to the highest honours. These four, the two sisters Braun, Kaltenbrunner and Fegelein, were amongst the most dangerous in the circle surrounding Hitler. In the final phase Kaltenbrunner spent several hours every day with the Führer, and did all he could to work him up to continue the course upon which he had embarked so long ago.

Among the principal actors of the Third Reich in the last act was also Reichsleiter Martin Bormann, the successor of Rudolf Hess, a man who had a very great influence over Hitler. He specialized in intrigues, but he also possessed another talent which he found very useful, the ability to reduce complicated matters to the simplest forms in his reports to Hitler. This was a talent which the Führer warmly appreciated.

Goebbels, who drew strength from his own speeches, who never ceased to be fascinated by them, even after practically everybody had ceased to believe what he said, and who from his safe shelter issued fiery orations exhorting the population of Berlin to fight to the last man; Göring, who from what one hears, after 1940 could never be shaken in his belief that Germany had definitely won the war and who, in this belief, allowed the Luftwaffe to deteriorate rapidly; Ribbentrop in his stupid conceit and his narrow views – all these belonged to the inner circle of those near Hitler in the end. Göring seems, however, to have ceased to have any influence.

And then there was Heinrich Himmler. In this connection, one can only remark that he appears to have been just as terrified of Hitler as Hitler was of Himmler. The intimate circle round Hitler directed all their plottings particularly against the Head of the Gestapo. As a result he was sent to the front, at first, in the late autumn of 1944, to the Western Front, and thereafter to the Oder Front. The Oder Front was one of the most dangerous and most exposed sections. The idea was that Himmler would fail there. He was to be discredited and afterwards 'liquidated'.

Himmler ended as a suicide, but not before Hitler had been 'liquidated'.

Shortly after the curtain had gone down on the drama of the European war, I had a long conversation with Minister Schellenberg, who, as already related, had come to Stockholm to arrange the surrender of the German troops in Norway, and who still remained in the Swedish capital. Because of my earlier connections with Schellenberg it was necessary for me to have a final conference with him. Owing to his opposition to the official policy Schellenberg had felt impelled to support my plans in connection with the Red Cross. And it can be said that the manner in which he exerted his influence at the end contributed in no small degree to Denmark and Norway being spared the horrors of destructive fighting. The decision that the German troops should surrender unconditionally was largely due to his energetic insistence.

Now Schellenberg was sitting with me telling me of his experiences during the final stage. He also gave me an insight into what went on behind the scenes in connection with my appearance on the German stage. His account, for the accuracy of which he himself must be responsible, appeared to me, from the point of view of history, and as supplementing my own impressions, to be of so great an interest that the main points should be given publicity.

Schellenberg's Story

To begin with (Schellenberg said), I should like to mention a period which was very significant. In 1943 Switzerland suddenly appeared in the very foreground of the political interests of the Reich. An attack upon Switzerland very nearly occurred. All plans had been prepared and approved by Ribbentrop and Bormann, and the military–political situation produced by the Allied landing in Italy seemed to make such an attack necessary. I opposed these plans tooth and nail, partly by attempting to contact certain friends of mine in Switzerland. Finally the idea was abandoned, mainly because of economic considerations. But Switzerland was certainly very near sharing the fate of Denmark and Norway and all the other occupied countries. The whole episode was very typical of the foreign policy of the Third Reich.

This was only one of the occasions when I attempted to actively oppose the official policy. After I had become Head of the Political

Department of the German Intelligence Service and, in 1944, Head of the whole organization, the defects of the régime became apparent to me. The upper strata were corrupt through and through. In my opinion the one exception was the Head of the SS, Himmler. As I became filled with the conviction that the policy directed by Hitler and Ribbentrop must lead to catastrophic results, it became clear to me that it was a matter of life and death for Germany that a counter-balance to this should be created. It was my belief that the only one who could do this was Himmler. It was in this spirit that I attempted to approach him and to obtain such an influence over him that his power should be directed in the way I desired. It was my conviction that Germany must in one way or another get out of the war with the Western Powers.

However strange it may sound, there was at the time of my appointment no real Political Intelligence Service in the Third Reich. And there was even less understanding of its importance. It was looked upon as superfluous, for the simple reason that the Third Reich did not require information about the interior situation in other countries; the Third Reich could do without that. This opinion was shared by Hitler, who was completely opposed to me in regard to this, as was also Ribbentrop. The only one who showed some interest was Himmler, but even he created difficulties for me, enslaved, as he was, by the prejudices created by the basic ideas of National Socialism, as well as his tendency to consider political events with the mind of a police official. It was only by slow degrees that I was able to produce a change in his attitude.

As the military and political situation became more critical my position became more difficult. I became the object of especial notice and interest on the part of the Gestapo and the Security Police. My most active and dangerous enemies were Reichs-leiter Bormann and the Head of the Security Police, Kaltenbrunner. It was especially in regard to Kaltenbrunner that I had to show great caution. As far back as eighteen months previously he stated that he had complete evidence that I was employed by the Secret Service (i.e. the British Secret Service). He did all in his power to trap me.

This was the situation when, in the beginning of February, the German Minister in Stockholm, Thomsen, reported that you were about to depart for Berlin in order to see Himmler. Twice that day Ribbentrop sent his personal secretary in the

Ministry for Foreign Affairs, Geheimerat Wagner, to see me in order to endeavour to find out if it was I who, through my personal connections in Sweden, had taken the initiative in arranging this journey. Ribbentrop and Kaltenbrunner regarded me as responsible for the pardoning and liberation of the seven so-called 'Warsaw Swedes', and tried to show that my intervention in this case, especially in view of the hostility of the Swedish press towards Germany, was a great political blunder. In a general way they did everything they could to inflame Hitler's antipathy to Sweden, particularly by giving him reports about the training of Norwegian policemen in Sweden.

I told Wagner, what was the truth, that I had no knowledge of your projected visit, and informed Himmler as well as Kaltenbrunner about these conversations. Himmler was interested but also annoyed that the arrangements for your journey should go through the Legation in Stockholm, and consequently through the Ministry for Foreign Affairs. This meant that he must treat your visit as being of an official nature and report it to Hitler. He therefore instructed Kaltenbrunner to make use of a favourable opportunity to mention the matter to Hitler and to try to ascertain what his feelings were. Instead Kaltenbrunner asked Gruppenführer Fegelein to attend to the matter, and the following day the latter was in a position to report that the Führer was definitely opposed to the project. 'Buffoonery of that kind won't help us in this war,' was Hitler's comment.

And then you arrived in Berlin. I at once telephoned to Himmler and begged him earnestly not to ignore this gesture on the part of Sweden, and said that he absolutely must receive you. After a great many objections Himmler agreed that Kaltenbrunner should speak to Ribbentrop and I to Geheimerat Wagner and try to arrange for Ribbentrop to see you without Hitler's knowledge, and without letting Ribbentrop know that the Führer had forbidden your reception. If Ribbentrop agreed, then I and Kaltenbrunner could also see you, and in this way Himmler would gain time and see how things developed.

This is how Kaltenbrunner and I were able to see you. From the very beginning I had a feeling that I had made a useful contact. I saw in your visit the last opportunity of realizing what had always been at the back of my mind: in some way or other to steer Germany out of the war. I also determined that a meeting between you and Himmler must be arranged, and as soon as you left me I set about it in the following manner.

I complimented Kaltenbrunner on the remarkable way in which he had conducted his conversation with you – a perfect example of Austrian 'Ballhaus diplomacy'. There was something which I had for a long time wanted to say to him, and which I had now decided to raise in the course of my next meeting with Himmler, and this was that, in the present desperate situation, Ribbentrop must be removed, and Kaltenbrunner appointed Minister for Foreign Affairs in his place. Kaltenbrunner swallowed the bait so readily and with such enthusiasm that I found it difficult to control the situation. When we then telephoned to Himmler, Kaltenbrunner insisted with burning conviction how essential it was that you should meet him, even though Hitler had definitely forbidden it. When your meeting took place Kaltenbrunner was not asked to attend, which made him furious. He sobered down and soon showed himself as hostile to me as ever. After your first meeting with Himmler the intrigues began again. Kaltenbrunner heaped reproaches on me because I had made the Reichsleiter altogether too well disposed to you, and enlisted the services of

Gruppenführer Muller, the brutal acting Chief of the Gestapo, who made every kind of objection to the plan to collect the Norwegian and Danish prisoners in Neuengamme. Among other objections he said that the German population, especially the long trains of refugees, must not be subjected to the sight of Swedish Red Cross cars driving about the roads at night with prisoners from the concentration camps. I would, however, not give in, but visited Himmler at his Headquarters and had it out with him. I told him that it was evident that Germany was about to collapse, and that in this situation he must in all circumstances make the most of your presence in Germany. I said that he must try to act independently in order to steer the German wreck into a peaceful haven before it capsized, and suggested that he should ask you to fly to General Eisenhower and present him with an offer of surrender.

The talk became more and more emotional as it went on. I said that Himmler's place should be in Berlin and not with an army group. It was the second time that Hitler's entourage had succeeded in getting him away from the capital, and that he should without any loss of time return there to prepare for peace, with or without using force. At last Himmler gave way, and that night I received very wide powers to negotiate with you. However the next morning he rang me up and took back most of what he had said, and only authorized me to maintain contact with you, and in certain circumstances to try to persuade you to see Eisenhower on your own initiative. From that day, in the beginning of March, there was a daily tug-of-war between Himmler and me, although neither Kaltenbrunner nor any of the other persons in Hitler's entourage were really aware of it.

In long talks with Himmler I tried to show him that there was no longer a question of being true to his oath to Hitler, who, as he always himself maintained, was the real basis of the SS organization, but that it was a matter of life and death for the German people. His reply was always, 'Then what you want me to do is to eliminate the Führer?' There was a time when I couldn't answer this question in the affirmative, for if I had, I ran the risk of being 'liquidated'. The influence possessed by Gruppenführer Fegelein, Obergruppenführer Kaitenbrunner, Obersturmbannführer Skorzeny, the Chief of the 'Werewolves', and others of their kind was so great, especially as it rested principally on their right to report personally to Hitler.

During these talks Himmler often spoke to me about the state of Hitler's health, which according to him was becoming worse from day to day. When I asked him how it was that he still possessed such power, Himmler said that his energy continued undiminished. He said that his abnormal way of life, his habit of turning night into day, and only sleeping two or three hours, his restless activity and continual outbursts of rage, completely exhausted those near him and made the whole atmosphere unbearable. I suggested that the attempt on his life of July 20th may have seriously affected his health, particularly the injuries to his head, and Himmler thought this possible, but he pointed out the significance of Hitler's stooping more and more, his slack appearance, and the marked tremor in his left arm.

It was in connection with these reports – personally I had not seen Hitler for a long time – that I, in the beginning of April, spoke to a friend of mine, Professor de Crinis, Head of the Psychiatric Section of the Charité Hospital. In answer to my questions he replied that he had observed in photographs in illustrated papers that Hitler's movements appeared almost paralyzed, and that he must regard this as a symptom of Parkinson's disease

(*Paralysis agitans*). I thereupon arranged a meeting between Himmler and de Crinis to which the Reichsleiter summoned the Reichsminister of Health, Conti. It was evident that Himmler was extremely interested by what he heard.

A few days later, it was April 13th, Himmler summoned me to his headquarters in Wustrow and took me for a walk in the forest, where he at last completely unburdened himself to me. 'Schellenberg,' he said, 'I don't think that we can let the Führer go on any longer. Do you believe that de Crinis was right?' I answered, 'Yes, it is true that it is two or three years since I met Hitler, but from what I can judge of his behaviour in recent times, I am convinced that it is high time for you to act.'

But after a while Himmler's vacillation began again. It was clear that the breach between him and Hitler had commenced. Over and over he asked me what he could do. He said that after all he could not murder the Führer, he could not give him poison, nor could he arrest him in the Reich Chancellory, for in that case the whole military machine would come to a stop. I replied that this would not matter. There was only one way out. He must present himself before Hitler, inform him of everything that had happened recently, and force him to abdicate. Himmler said that this was absolutely impossible, as the Führer would burst into an attack of rage and shoot him on the spot. 'You must take suitable precautions to prevent this,' I said. 'After all, you have a sufficient number of SS men in high positions who are capable of arranging an arrest of this kind. If there is no other way we must get the doctors to help.'

Our walk went on for an hour and a half. Himmler was not able to come to a decision, but only said that he would arrange a meeting between Professor de Crinis, Professor Morell, Hitler's body physician, Dr. Stumpfegger, his other physician, and Bormann.

A couple of days later, I asked Professor de Crinis what conclusion he and his colleagues had reached. He answered rather disappointedly that he had discussed with Dr. Stumpfegger principally the supposed symptoms of Parkinson's disease. Stumpfegger had not shared his opinion, although he had to accept some of his points. In the end they had agreed about certain medicines, which he had had prepared in his clinic, but Stumpfegger had not called for them; he himself had had the intention of procuring medicines. 'There was therefore the possibility that Stumpfegger had no intention of fetching the medicines in de Crinis's clinic. I reported this to Himmler who begged me insistently to keep this matter entirely to myself.

During the days which followed my walk with Himmler on April 13th, events began to move in the direction I had long anticipated. During the first week in April I got into touch with the Minister for Finance, Count Schwerin von Krosigk. In the course of long talks we agreed that the war must be brought to an end in order to save as much of Germany as possible. In connection with these talks I arranged a meeting for April 19th between Himmler and von Krosigk. Relations between these two men had been broken off for a long time. Before the meeting Himmler was extremely strung up and at the last moment wanted to cancel it. However, it took place in the presence of Reichsarbeitsminister Seldte, who had at one time been the leader of the Stahlhelm Party. During the meeting von Krosigk talked with Himmler while I conferred with Seldte. The latter was of the opinion that Himmler must take the leadership and compel Hitler to read a proclamation to the German people on the occasion of his birthday, in which it should be announced that a plebiscite would be held, a new party formed and the People's Courts abolished.

After the conference von Krosigk informed me that he had discussed with Himmler all the questions which we had gone over, and earnestly entreated him to act against the Führer. Himmler thanked me for having arranged a meeting with the Minister of Finance. I replied that in my opinion von Krosigk was the only person whom he could make Ribbentrop's successor as Minister for Foreign Affairs. Himmler agreed with me, but thereupon began to speak about the Allies' propaganda against himself in connection with the concentration camps. 'The whole thing is senseless. It won't in any case make any difference to me, but you must not believe in this propaganda; it isn't true.'

I cannot describe the events of the following days in detail. Hitler's birthday passed uneventfully. On April 21st you had another meeting with Himmler. During this time Himmler complained to me that his health was not any too good, and I noticed how nervy and anxious he was. 'Schellenberg,' he said to me on one occasion, 'I am filled with horror at the thought of what is now coming.' Another time he told me what he would do when power was in his hands. He requested me the same evening to propose a name for the new party which it had been suggested to him he should found. I suggested to him 'Party of National Unity'. Himmler then took up the question of the 'liquidation' of Hitler, but only in terms of vague allusions.

The night of April 23rd–24th there was another meeting between you and Himmler in Lübeck, when he asked you to present an offer of surrender to the Western Powers, this to be transmitted through the Swedish Government. It was then that he said that it could only be 'a question of one, two, or, at most, three days, before the Führer ends his dynamic life in this dramatic struggle.'

According to my calculations the life of the Führer ended on April 27th, and it is my definite belief that it was by means of an injection. However, I do not know who it was who gave it to him.

The events in Berlin on the following day, April 28th, are probably not generally known. It is certain, however, that Grand Admiral Dönitz's nomination as Hitler's successor took place on the 29th. There are also fairly certain grounds for believing that it was Reichsleiter Bormann who made the nomination. It was the last move against Himmler. Himmler realized that capitulation was unavoidable and for this reason he was pushed aside.

In the meanwhile I was continuing my negotiations with you and with Himmler. My endeavours were in the first place to bring about a peaceful solution of the Danish and Norwegian problem, in order that Germany should not be further burdened with the senseless destruction of the Scandinavian countries. On April 29th I accompanied you to Copenhagen to negotiate with, among others, Dr. Best, and then, as you know, immediately returned to Germany. When I arrived at the place where Himmler was I was informed that not he, but Dönitz, had been nominated Hitler's successor, and that same night the first conference between Hammler and Dönitz had taken place at Plön, and that the Reichsleiter, in accordance with my earlier proposal, had succeeded in obtaining the nomination of Schwerin von Krosigk as Ribbentrop's successor. Himmler was very depressed, for in the army, too, there was no real appreciation or understanding of his struggle to obtain an agreement with the Western Powers about capitulation. Himmler was now considering whether he should resign and commit suicide, but wanted to discuss the situation once more with me.

Some hectic and nerve-racking days followed, without sleep and with difficult and dangerous motor drives through the actual battle zone. When I, in Himmler's company, on May 1st, for the first time arrived at Dönitz's headquarters at Plön, I found, there, a very tense atmosphere. It was soon apparent that von Krosigk held the same views as Himmler and I, while Dönitz as well as Keitel and Jodl – that is, the leading commanders – were at that time under no circumstances prepared to give up Norway without a fight. They particularly pointed out that the German commander in Norway, Colonel-General Böhme, was in a very strong strategic position.

The negotiations continued. For a long time Dönitz hesitated to agree to von Krosigk's and my proposals. In the end I was appointed envoy with instructions to conduct negotiations in Stockholm about the surrender of the troops in Norway. As for the events from then until May 7th, they are known to you.

Thus far Schellenberg. As I listened to him the many impressions of the last months flashed through my mind. I had received further confirmation of the opinion to which I gave expression on my return home from one of my latest voyages to Germany. I said at that time: 'I return to Sweden as an even greater opponent of the Nazi creed than before, but at the same time cannot help having a deep feeling of sympathy for Germany's unhappy People.' They have failed. They have allowed themselves to be led by ruthless scoundrels. They must drain the cup of suffering. But as the representative of an organization of the humanitarian character of the Red Cross, I must urge that afterwards they shall be helped and led on to other paths, not with hatred and brutality, but by people who realize that love is the strongest power for good. Then, and then only, can we after the downfall of the Third Reich look forward to a happier world for cruelly tried humanity.